THE REAL
TRUTH ABOUT
TEENS & SEX

THE REAL TRUTH ABOUT TEENS & SEX

From Hooking Up to Friends with Benefits—
What Teens Are Thinking, Doing,
and Talking About, and How to Help Them
Make Smart Choices

Sabrina Weill

A Perigee Book

THE BERKLEY PUBLISHING GROUP
Published by the Penguin Group
Penguin Group (USA) Inc.
375 Hudson Street, New York, New York 10014, USA
Penguin Group (Canada), 90 Eglinton Avenue East, Suite 700, Toronto, Ontario M4P 2Y3, Canada
(a division of Pearson Penguin Canada Inc.)
Penguin Books Ltd., 80 Strand, London WC2R 0RL, England
Penguin Group Ireland, 25 St. Stephen's Green, Dublin 2, Ireland (a division of Penguin Books
Ltd.)
Penguin Group (Australia), 250 Camberwell Road, Camberwell, Victoria 3124, Australia
(a division of Pearson Australia Group Pty. Ltd.)
Penguin Books India Pvt. Ltd., 11 Community Centre, Panchsheel Park, New Delhi—110 017,
India
Penguin Group (NZ), Cnr. Airborne and Rosedale Roads, Albany, Auckland 1310, New Zealand
(a division of Pearson New Zealand Ltd.)
Penguin Books (South Africa) (Pty.) Ltd., 24 Sturdee Avenue, Rosebank, Johannesburg 2196,
South Africa

Penguin Books Ltd., Registered Offices: 80 Strand, London WC2R 0RL, England

This book is an original publication of The Berkley Publishing Group.

Copyright © by Sabrina Weill, 2005
Text design by Tiffany Estreicher.

First Perigee hardcover edition: September 2005

Library of Congress Cataloging-in-Publication Data
Weill, Sabrina Solin.
     The real truth about teens and sex : from hooking up to friends with benefits : what teens are
doing, thinking, and talking about, and how to help them make smart choices / Sabrina Weill.
         p. cm.
     Includes bibliographical references and index.
     ISBN 0-399-53198-X
     1. Teenagers—Sexual behavior.   2. Sexual ethics for teenagers.   I. Title.

HQ27.W445 2005
306.7'0835—dc22

                                                                                2005048937

PRINTED IN THE UNITED STATES OF AMERICA

10   9   8   7   6   5   4   3   2

For Steven,

Jack, and Amelia:

you inspire me.

Contents

THE REAL TRUTH ABOUT TEENS & SEX

"I Have Something to Tell You . . ."

The idea for this book began the day I learned about chicken parties.

It was a cold winter morning, and I was editor-in-chief of *Seventeen*. I was working on the last few stories of an issue when an editor came into my office waving a letter. "Have you ever heard of chicken parties?" she asked. I hadn't. She explained that at these parties teen girls would perform oral sex on teen guys, all in a group. "Chicken parties" were so named because of the bobbing of the girls' heads. Awful, yes. One letter doesn't make a trend though, so we waited. And more e-mails came, talking about these chicken parties.

THE STORY UNFOLDS . . .
The more I mentioned "chicken parties" to parents, the more the stories came out: someone had heard about them happening at a cousin's kid's sweet sixteen, at a son's birthday party, at a house when the parents were out of town. . . . My friend's uncle who lived in California and had teenage sons had heard of these parties. My friend who is an adolescent counselor in a small town in New Jersey had heard of them ("That's nothing," she said, "at the middle school here they play *Smile*—where the girls duck under a table that boys are sitting at, and the first boy to smile loses").

A few weeks later, this editor was on the subway and she saw a group of teen girls. She introduced herself as a teen magazine editor and asked them: "Have you ever heard of chicken parties?" The girls nodded and giggled. "Oh yeah," they said. "We've heard of them."

Now, this felt like a trend. Girls were clearly at least talking about oral sex in general and about party hookups in particular.

So I ran the story, "Oral Report," in the magazine. The story explained what we were hearing and in no uncertain terms advised girls strongly not to engage in casual intimacy. One of the benefits of having a huge national platform like *Seventeen* is you can advocate for teens and, yes, you get to publicize your point of view. I'm generally not judgmental and feel it's always been my job to inform teens rather than advise them on what to do—I believe that given all the information and support, the vast majority of teens can make intelligent decisions. That said, it is my firm belief (and I'm sure, every parent's) that having so-called party sex is bad for teens, and it's especially bad for girls, who tend to report damaged reputations and a good deal of regret.

READERS REACT

After the story came out, I waited for the onslaught of angry-adult letters that I was sure would accuse us of indoctrinating girls into a free-sex lifestyle. No matter how clear or responsible an article is, the mention of sex in a teen magazine is certain to ignite a given amount of agita in people who would rather not believe that teens are engaging in these kinds of activities. To my surprise, I only got a few of those letters. But I got many e-mails from girls saying various versions of, "Hey, this is happening at my school, and thanks so much for writing about it because now I know what to do if I ever end up at a party where this is going on—I don't want to feel bad about myself and now I know I can just say I'm not into this and leave."

The exciting thing about this story is that I was in a position to listen to teens, reflect their reality to them, and then give them the information they needed to make smart choices. If you're a parent, you probably recognize this as your primary responsibility. Throughout

my career I've heard from thousands of teens and also dozens of parents, who often come up to me at events or lunches, grab my elbow, and whisper, "Tell me what's going on with my kid—I don't understand him/her anymore, she/he seems to hate me, and what's this I keep reading about SEX PARTIES?!?"

You've probably read a lot about teens and sex in the past year, because you either have a teenager or you care very much about teenagers—enough to want to help them make some of the most important decisions in their lives very carefully and thoughtfully. So, you and I have that in common. I've dedicated more than a decade to helping teenagers learn more about themselves and helping them have the confidence to make the best possible choices.

A LITTLE ABOUT ME

I began my career at *Seventeen* as an editorial assistant. Then, as an associate editor, I wrote my first book: *The Seventeen Guide to Sex and Your Body*. Next I was senior editor, then editor-in-chief, of the Scholastic magazines *Choices* and *Health Choices*. I was the founding executive editor of *CosmoGIRL!* magazine and was in that role for nearly 4 years before I was hired back to *Seventeen* as editor-in chief. Throughout this time, I received as many as several hundred e-mails a day from teens across the country. Every month, at each of these magazines, our staff editors would read hundreds, sometimes thousands, of e-mails and letters. We'd bring them to meetings and let the readers inspire our story ideas and the tone and spirit of the magazine. Often I'd write readers back myself to thank them for their thoughts or to ask them to clarify something they'd said. Each time they'd be so appreciative, and very often their response would start with "Thanks so much for actually reading my letter—for listening to me."

For the past few years, while I've been doing all this listening-to-teens, I've been granted a rare inside pass to their world. Because teens know I am not a psychologist, not a teacher, not their parent—I'm more like a professional older sister—they know I am not interested in judging them. All I ask of them is their honesty. And whenever I've had the opportunity to talk to teens, individually or through editor's letters or articles I've written, I've always tried to be as honest as I can with them, and I know this has resonated with them because they tell me so. Teens are so used to being judged, marginalized, and talked down to that they quickly identify adults who don't do these things. They often write me e-mails saying, "Thanks for being so *real.*" I feel grateful that time and time again, through their letters, calls, and in-person chats, they've let me into their world. It is with this knowledge that I offer you a glimpse into teens' innermost thoughts and feelings about this difficult subject.

CONNECTING TEENS AND ADULTS

I have often been asked for advice about how to get teens to open up, what to say and what not to say, and what teens are really up to these days—because as you probably know or suspect, the vast majority of teens are actually *not* participating in sex parties. But teens nationwide *are* suffering from a lack of honest communication from their parents and other pivotal adults around them on this topic, and far too many teens are still engaging in risky, early sex and enduring the consequences of unwanted pregnancy and STDs. Knowing this, I decided I'd write for the audience that could be most helpful to teens: adults who care passionately about them and want nothing more than to help teenagers become healthy, successful adults. And so, the idea for this book.

I set up a website and asked all my media contacts to publicize it—it was mentioned in a wide range of websites and newsletters, from huge sites like seventeen.com to smaller sites like purplepjs.com. I wrote an open letter to teens, explaining that I wanted to write a book that would tell the truth about what was really going on with teens and sex—and to help parents and other adults communicate better with teens about sex.

The response was amazing: thousands of teens from all across the country came to the site, and hundreds of thousands more received my letter via e-mail. Hundreds of teens agreed to tell me what's going on with dating, love, and sex in their hometowns. A wide variety of organizations dedicated to informing teens agreed to send my letter to subscribers of their newsletters—including the more than 4,000-teen Youth Online Network of The National Campaign to Prevent Teen Pregnancy. After each new wave of publicity, I was inundated with new teen voices.

"THANKS FOR LISTENING"

Many of the teens who contacted me repeated the same sentiment: "Thanks for giving me this opportunity to tell you about these things—thanks for listening." It reinforced my feeling that teens are eager to be honest, to be open, and to have an opportunity to relate to adults. Even though it doesn't always seem like it, teenagers *want* to talk to us about their sex lives. "I have so many things to share with you," said Sadie, 14, from New Jersey. "Thank you! Someone cares what I have to say about dating!" And Kelly, 16, from New York, said: "I read about your upcoming book on the Internet, and I think what you're doing to make adults more aware of today's teenage dating scene is wonderful." Please note that though I've edited their words very little, all the names and some identifying details of the teens and parents in this book have been changed to protect their privacy. Because this book addresses issues concerning teen boys and girls, I've used both male and female pronouns throughout. And though this book is for parents, teachers, health educators, and everyone who cares about teens, I'm going to use "your teen" throughout to refer to the teen or teens you personally are most concerned with.

A REALITY-BASED LOOK AT TEENS

The goal of this book is to present parents and other concerned adults with a realistic picture of what today's teens are thinking, feeling, talking about and doing vis-à-vis dating and sex. I'm also offering specific scripts that will help adults start the kinds of conversations that guide teens to make intelligent decisions. I spoke to our nation's foremost experts on this topic, from school counselors and adolescent gynecologists to leading university researchers and the authors of the newest studies and research on teens and sex. All this information helped me show what teens are really up to (both with anecdotal and scientific evidence) and give concrete advice so adults can communicate more effectively with teens. All experts and scientific evidence point to this solid fact: when parents (and other central adults in their lives) connect with and communicate clearly with teens about sex and sexuality, the teens make smarter, more responsible choices.

I also had the thrilling opportunity to be advised by experts at The National Campaign to Prevent Teen Pregnancy as I created a survey that was fielded to a nationally representative sample of teens age 12 to 17. In September 2004, 1,059 teens were interviewed by Ipsos, a leading market research company, via a 10-minute online survey; the results were tabulated in March 2005. (The teens' parents were allowed to view the survey content, but then the parents were asked to agree to allow their child privacy while responding so the teens would answer the questions openly and honestly.) The results, "Teens Tell the Truth! Teens Talk Honestly About Sex, Love, and Relationships," are revealed for the first time in this book—they're labeled "Tell the Truth!" (For more details about the survey, go to www.sabrinaweill.com.) I've also included some of the more than 800 responses to the question, "What was the one thing your parents said to you that had the most impact on your decision about virginity?" You'll see these responses sprinkled throughout the book under the heading "I listened when my parents said . . ."

In creating this book, I communicated with hundreds of teens, dozens of incredibly knowledgeable experts, and many open and caring parents. I gathered all these insightful anecdotes and fantastic advice and some great ideas about what needed to be said and how to say it. I also had my own experience to draw upon—after writing and editing hundreds of articles for teenagers, I have a good sense of what will and won't play with teens. (Teens are great about letting you know when an idea you thought was genius is, in fact, "stupid.") I'd produced a national survey, and the results were fascinating and telling. *This would be easy,* I thought to myself. *I can't wait to lay out all this information and start really showing everyone what teens are actually up to—and helping with the crucial task of talking to teens about sex.*

"ALL TEENAGERS" / "MY TEENAGER"

Then, the week before I started to write the manuscript, my family spent a weekend with friends who have teenage daughters with whom I am extremely close. I walked into the den while they were chatting with their dad about guys.

"I know guys," their father was saying. "You can always ask me anything." The girls just giggled. "Sabrina," said Rebecca (who's 15 and would be horrified if I used her real name), "your daughter is so lucky because you've worked at a magazine, so she'll feel comfortable asking you anything about guys and sex and stuff like that." I knew this was the moment I'd been writing about, when the teen opens the door and the adult is supposed to say, "Yes—ask me anything! I'll always give you the information you need." But I looked at Rebecca, in her running shorts and newly unbraced teeth and thick gorgeous hair that she sometimes still wears in braids, and I thought about some pimply-faced teenage guy putting his hands on her and felt physically sick. And worse yet, I choked! I blurted out something awkward like, "Yeah, well, it's way too soon for you to be thinking about this stuff, heh heh." Then I fled from the room.

A little while later, I composed myself. While we were chopping vegetables together in the kitchen, I told my teen friend's mom what had happened and got her blessing to re-approach Rebecca. And then I did let Rebecca know that in no uncertain terms, I would answer any questions she ever had on this topic and any other topic. I said it fast, but I said it clearly, and I reiterated it a few times after that during various phone conversations. As a result, we've had several honest talks on this topic and I've been able to give her information I know will help her make smarter decisions. I tell you this story because I want you to know that I realize that "teenagers" are different from "*my* teenager," and it's with that sensitivity in mind that I offer you the real-world advice in this book. Please know that even though you might not want to use the exact scripts I offer as a guide (in the "Talk the Talk" sections) and you might not feel comfortable talking about some of these topics, anything you can say is a step in the right direction and any help you can offer teenagers will have a huge impact on them and their decisions.

FROM "HOOKING UP" TO "FWB" AND EVERYTHING IN BETWEEN

So in each chapter of this book, I'm going to explain what I see as the major issues in teens' sex lives today and provide plenty of teen testimony so you can see how these issues are playing out in a middle school or high school near you. I imagine that some of the teens in here will remind you in some way of teens you know, and because these kids were speaking very candidly to me, you may get a glimpse at another side of your teen's life. I'll offer hard evidence about what's really happening, both in the form of first-person teen stories and statistics. Many of these statistics were culled from organizations and researchers who are devoted to doing crucial work that helps teenagers make smart choices in this realm such as the Centers for Disease Control and Prevention (CDC), the Alan Guttmacher Institute, Child Trends, The National Campaign to Prevent Teen Pregnancy, and many others, as well as, of course, from the Truth Survey results.

REAL-WORLD ADVICE

Finally, in each chapter I'll offer what I call "Real-World Advice." As someone who has worked for magazines for more than a decade, I can tell you that I usually don't like to read articles or books that purport to give me advice, because the advice is almost never good. Magazine articles and experts almost always give advice that's kind of easy to say and generally sounds too good to be true because it *is* (like "If you do these three things in the next five minutes, your presently overwhelming life crisis will be solved—forever!"). That's why, whenever I give advice, I always run it past a panel of experts—like real-life teens and their parents. I've talked about all the advice in here with my parents-of-teens panel (a revolving group of parents, counselors, and other adults who work with teens—individually they sometimes struggle with and other times excel at having these kinds of conversations), so I can assure you that the advice in here is grounded in reality, and it really works.

HELPING TEENS MAKE SMART CHOICES

Speaking of my panel, every time I checked in with them they would say, "Please hurry up and *finish* this book already—I need it!" which is so flattering because I know they're trusting me to give advice on this very important and delicate topic. I realize that unless you're a teacher or a health professional your sample size of teens may be a few teens, whereas mine was, at my last position, more than 10 million teenagers strong. Even though I've corresponded with thousands of teens, however, I don't know *your* teen.

But I do know this: one thing all "my teens" as well as the experts and clinical research data point to, is that we have the power to have an enormous influence on our teens' behavior—a fact that most of us accept with almost equal parts of relief and responsibility. So if you read this book and "Talk the Talk" with your teenager, your teenager *will* know you care deeply about him or her, and about this issue, and your teen absolutely *will* make smarter decisions about sex. So it's my hope that you'll read the teen voices in here, maybe recognize a little bit of your teen (or your teen-to-be) in some of the stories, and use the advice to help you open up communication between yourself and the teenager or teenagers you care so deeply about. I know you won't regret it.

—Sabrina Weill

PS: If you have a communication success story or advice for other parents, teachers, or health professionals who work with teens; want to join my parents-of-teens panel; or want to tell me your thoughts on the topics covered in this book, please go to www.sabrinaweill.com or e-mail me at sabrinaweill@aol.com.

TRUTH #1

Teens Have **Secrets** About Sex (and They Want Adults to Know Them)

✳ **Exclusive National Survey Results** ✳
Teens: Tell the Truth!

Do you have a secret about your sex life
that you'd never tell your parents?

1 in 11   14-year-olds say YES.

1 in 8   15-year-olds say YES.

1 in 5   16-year-olds say YES.

1 in 3   17-year-olds say YES.

"We lie to you because we don't want to disappoint you . . . or get yelled at."
—Bethany, 17, New Jersey

Many parents have confessed to me that, at some point, they have experienced a nearly irrepressible urge to rifle through their teen's backpack. Or to read their teen's journal—be it an online diary or a lined book filled with loopy script that was left spread-eagle and spine-up near the family computer . . . practically emblazoned with "Read me—she'll never notice."

It's understandable that parents would want to do a little investigating. Even without any solid evidence or direct testimony, there are clues when a teen is embarking on a journey for which his or her parents did *not* plan the itinerary: the left-onscreen IM to a girl with an unfamiliar name that ends "i luv u!" or a thong underwear in the wash that was not a parent-endorsed purchase. Even though we know teens have a social life that frequently doesn't include adult supervision, the oft-sudden realization that they may be hiding such an important part of their lives can be a startling wake-up call.

Just as a teenager's life gets more complicated, the stakes get higher: heartbreak, STDs, and pregnancy become immediate risks. At the same time, from a developmental standpoint, teens are supposed to be pulling away from the adults in their lives. In a sense, this pulling-away is good for both parents and teens: it's one thing to be an 11-year-old's main confidante, but no parent truly wants a play-by-play of their 15-year-old's date, any more than a teen wants to know the details of his or her parent's romantic life.

But at the same time, many teens do not have the maturity, judgment, or sophistication to make possibly life-changing decisions regarding sex without the input of an older, wiser adult. So, that's the bind we find ourselves in, needing to: 1 See what's truly going on in teens' sex lives and 2 Talk to teens about sex and sexuality in a way that will empower them to confidently make intelligent, responsible decisions (even though they act like they don't want to talk to us at all, let alone about sex). On the front lines of this communication gap, many parents and other adults who care about teens have pulled me aside to ask, "What's going on with my teenager? I found this [thong underwear/love letter/condom], and I'm not sure what it means. Is my teen in love? Or in danger? Or both? Help!"

And I think I *can* help—because teens confide in me. Ever since I began communicating with teens more than a decade ago as the "Sex and Body" columnist for *Seventeen* magazine, teens have been telling me what they consider to be their deepest, darkest secrets—secrets they are too afraid or too embarrassed to reveal to their parents, their teachers, or the adult in their lives they feel closest to. Often, these are secrets teens think adults can't handle. "What would happen," I sometimes ask, "if you told your parents what's really going on with you?"

> *"They'd freak out."*
> *"They'd kick me out of the house."*
> *"They wouldn't understand."*
> *"They don't know what it's like to be a teenager now."*

Even though I generally like to take a listen-without-judging approach to teens, this is the one place where teens so often get it wrong. Most of the parents I speak to want to know more about what's going on with their teen's life, not to persecute them or put them on "lockdown," but to help them.

TEENS WANT TO CLOSE THE COMMUNICATION GAP

As I was starting research for this book, I sent an e-mail to teens saying, "Listen, I know it can be hard to talk about sex, so if you tell me your secret thoughts, feelings, and actions, I'll share your words in a book, to help adults understand where you're coming from and how best to help you."

You might think teens would say, "No thanks! I'll keep my most intimate thoughts to myself if it's all the same to you." It is, after all, the rare teen (dare I say, *no* teen) who wants to break the news about what they're up to sexually to their own parents. This is, in part, because of the embarrassment factor. And anecdotal as well as scientific research (and good common sense) tells us that teens, like children of all ages, are loath to disappoint their parents.

✳ Exclusive National Survey Results ✳
Teens: Tell the Truth!

**53% of 12- to 17-year-olds are "very" or "extremely" concerned
about disappointing their parents.
Another 36% report they are "concerned."
8% are "a little concerned."
Only 3% are "not concerned at all."**

But they did confide in me: hundreds of teens contacted me, eager to share the most intimate details about their love and sex lives (or lack thereof) and stating quite explicitly that they *wanted* me to tell parents and other adults in their lives about their secret thoughts, their personal feelings, and even their most private actions. "I have to say, your book is a wonderful idea," said Melinda, 16, from Washington. "Many parents these days think they know what's going on with their kids. But they don't. So kudos to you for educating the 'rents on what's going on." So many teens express this sentiment to me in one way or another that it reinforces my belief that despite the horrified looks on their faces when we bring it up, teens *want* to discuss sex and sexuality with an adult they trust. They want parents know what's going on.

They just don't want to be the ones to bring it up.

WHAT'S REALLY GOING ON

You don't have to look too hard in your local paper, on the news, or yes, even in my e-mail inbox, to find panic-inducing stories about teens having group sex at parties or on buses or playing sex games and getting pregnant at tender ages—these rumors and trends are addressed in the next chapter. In this chapter, I want to provide the big picture: today's teen-sex landscape—what's going on with *most* teenagers across the country. These statistics and revelations are based on my interviews and contact with teenagers, as well as national surveys, including my nationwide Teens: Tell the Truth! survey of more than 1,000 teenagers, which I produced in consultation with The National Campaign to Prevent Teen Pregnancy, the results of which are revealed in this book for the first time.

Knowing the truth about teens and sex is the first step to helping teenagers sift through the ever-changing choices and vital decisions they will make in the coming years.

And, happily for both parents and teens, no one's diary will be read in the process.

GOOD NEWS FIRST

There is always plenty of negative news about teens behaving badly and how sexual and sexually active teens are today. But in truth, over the past 15 years some very positive trends concerning teens and sex have been evolving. For example:

✳ Positive Trends ✳

- **Teens are having less intercourse in high school (down 14% from 1991).**
- **Those teens who are having sex are using more contraception (91% of boys and 83% of girls who had sex in the 3 months prior to being surveyed used contraception.)**
- **Teen pregnancy is down 30% over the past decade.**

—CDC, 2004

And the most recent National Survey of Family Growth (a National Center for Health Statistics study that includes responses and interview information from thousands of teens) confirms that these positive trends are continuing. So even though the bad news about teens is often the loudest, it's not the only news to pay attention to.

Nationwide, just under half of all teenagers—46.7 percent—are sexually active, and in my conversations with teens over the past decade I have definitely noticed a culture shift from many teens telling me they feel it's "totally embarrassing" to be a virgin to a growing group of teens who are virgins and proud of it.

"I don't think it's cool to have sex"

"I go to a big suburban all-boys high school. I consider myself funny, helpful, and athletic. I'm into sports and hanging out with friends, at the movies and the mall.

"I think virginity is pretty important, but I know a lot of people who have already lost their virginity when they were in 8th grade. I know many more people who have lost it this year in 9th grade. I also know that many people who have had sex at our school don't tell people about it. I don't know why, maybe because they don't want their parents to end up finding out. I don't think it's cool to have sex. It's way too early, and I don't think we should. Yes I am a virgin, I have been offered to have sex, but I don't want to. It's too early, and I just don't want to take that chance of having a baby."   —Colby, 14, Missouri

The fact that more teens are choosing virginity is good news in part because the latest research about teen's brains shows that there are developmental reasons to encourage teens to delay sex. "Twelve, 13, 14 is absolutely too young," says Kristin Moore, Ph.D., who is a scholar and president of the Washington D.C.–based research organization Child Trends. "Kids are only developing formal operational thinking at 15 and 16." Teens' capacity to make smart decisions—decisions that will affect their future, including choices about contraception and STD prevention—are still forming. So it doesn't matter if parents value delaying sex until marriage, or until after high school, or until there is a committed and loving relationship in place . . . the longer a teenager delays sex, the more time she is giving her brain to catch up with her body, and the higher the chances are that she'll be able to make intelligent, careful decisions that will protect her from STDs and pregnancy when the time comes.

✳ What do teens think about teens ✳ being virgins?

81% of teens do not think teenagers should be sexually active.

–The National Campaign to Prevent Teen Pregnancy (NCTPTP), 2004

THE REST OF THE PICTURE

A good many teenagers are still having sex while in high school, and there is a sense among teens and the health educators I spoke to that more teens are holding off on having sex, but those who are sexually active are fooling around with more partners. And although there has been a decline in sexual activity among teens under 15, nearly one-third of ninth graders are still having sex.

✳ At what age are teens losing ✳ their virginity?

32.8% of 9th graders have had sex.

44.1% of 10th graders have had sex.

53.2% of 11th graders have had sex.

61.6% of 12th graders have had sex.

—CDC, 2003

Sexually active teens (much like sexually active adults) tend to fall into one of three camps: 1) Those who have sex once and then wait a long time—sometimes years—before they do it again. 2) Those who are in relationships and have sex either on occasion or frequently with their partner. 3) The smallest subset of all: teens who have sex frequently with multiple partners.

✳ How often are sexually active teens ✳ having sex?

Of sexually active boys ages 15 to 17:
86% had engaged in intercourse in the past year.
47% had engaged in intercourse in the past month.
36% had engaged in intercourse 10 or more times in the past year.
—Alan Guttmacher Institute, 2002

Though it's a minority, 14.4 percent of high school students have had sex with 4 or more partners—20.3 percent of 12th graders have done so. For obvious reasons, this statistic in particular gives pause to many people who dedicate their lives to helping teens avoid unplanned pregnancy and STDs.

"I've noticed a lot of hooking up"

"As a senior I've noticed a lot of people hooking up. Not just hooking up, but getting out of control with hooking up. They don't even feel one should have romance together to have sex with somebody. And the guys enjoy it. Nobody gets a bad reputation from it either. Word gets around quickly in my school about who's dating who and who's sleeping with you. There are groups of kids at my school who like to sleep around. Others, such as myself, believe there should be feelings, romance, and more between the couple to have sex."

—Josey, 17, New Jersey

When teenagers say "hooking up," it can mean anything from meeting at the mall to fooling around or having sexual intercourse, it's all in the context. Likewise, teenagers have a somewhat expanded definition of what it means to lose one's virginity:

✳ Teens: Tell the Truth! ✳

**Is someone who doesn't have sexual intercourse
but does do "everything but" still considered a virgin?
47% of 12 to 17-year-olds say YES
29% say NO
24% say they don't know**

It's interesting that nearly a quarter of teenagers seem unsure about what qualifies as virginity loss—this used to be a rather cut-and-dried issue. It speaks to the new and shifting boundaries and new ways of talking and thinking about sex that this is no longer the case. I will add, though, that in my experience when teens are talking about themselves (i.e.: "When I lost my virginity"), the term "virginity" does tend to mean sexual intercourse.

✳ How do teens define "sex"? ✳

**91% of teenagers age 13 to 16 agree that sexual intercourse
is sex
77% agree that oral sex is sex
45% agree that touching someone's genitals or
private parts is sex**
—NBC/People, 2004

The above statistics are in line with what I generally hear from teenagers. When they use the phrase "having sex," either in reference to themselves or others, they are often referring to sexual intercourse but they may also be talking about other sexual acts. But these definitions, like so many in the Teen Lexicon, are fluid—it's worth asking teenagers questions to confirm exactly what they're talking about. (Interestingly, sometimes the discovery is that the teenager himself is not sure.)

WHEN AND WHERE ARE TEENS HAVING SEX?

It is often commonly assumed that teens are having sex between 3 and 6 P.M., those unsupervised hours between school ending and parents coming home from work. But recent studies show that sex between teens generally takes place in the evening (after 6 P.M.) and that teens are usually having sex at home—two-thirds of teens in a National Longitudinal Survey of Youth reported having had sex at their own home, a partner's home, or a friend's home. Knowing this, I wondered how many parents were actually at home while these teens were fooling around. So I included that question in the Truth survey:

✳ Exclusive National Survey Results ✳
Teens: Tell the Truth!

Do you know a teen who has had sex at home
while their parents were in the house?
24% of 14-year-olds say YES.
42% of 15-year-olds say YES.
42% of 16-year-olds say YES.
60% of 17-year-olds say YES.

HOW CAN PARENTS TELL IF THEIR TEEN IS HAVING SEX?

Sure, these statistics are all very interesting—and right now parents may be rethinking that "open-door" policy that used to seem so restrictive but now suddenly sounds like a good idea. The number one question I get from parents is, "How can I tell if my teen is having sex?" Well, one way is to ask, but she may not tell you the truth (at the end of this chapter is real-world advice about not making it easy for teens to lie to you). Unless the parents and teen are extraordinarily close or the teen has sex for the first time when she's in her late teens, the parents probably won't get to know for sure exactly when it happens. Loss of virginity is just not something teens are necessarily motivated to share with their parents—they know this is news that will, in all likelihood, not be met with enthusiasm.

"If you want to know . . ."

"I'd love to let parents know that sex is everywhere, but that does not mean that your teenager has sex. If you want to know if your teenager is having sex, ask them; it's the only way to know. If we lie to you and give you the answer you want, it's because we don't want to disappoint you or... get yelled at.

"Teenagers are not all stupid, but all of us need help. I won't lie, sex is fun. We like to be sexy and have sex. So many teenagers are sexually active, but that does not mean they are ready for it. Don't hold back from 'the talk' or sharing information hoping that it will protect your children, because it only hurts them when they get the wrong information. Sex is everywhere, and we can't change that— we can only learn from it."   —Bethany, 17, New Jersey

Many of those teens who lie to their parents tell me they are doing so to protect their parents. Some say they don't want their parents to worry, while others say they just know their parents (especially the fathers of girls) would be really sad to know they are fooling around.

✳ Exclusive National Survey Results ✳
Teens: Tell the Truth!

28% of 12- to 17-year-olds agree that it's "always" or "sometimes" okay to lie to your parents about your sex life.

Still other teens tell me that while they wouldn't lie to their parents if asked outright, they're not offering up the information, either.

✳ Exclusive National Survey Results ✳
Teens: Tell the Truth!

Are you keeping a secret from your parents about whether you're sexually active?
1 in 13 15-year-olds say YES.

1 in 8 16-year-olds say YES.

1 in 5 17-year-olds say YES.

Hard as it may be for some parents to digest, from the standpoint of protecting teens, it doesn't matter if parents know exactly when they start having sex. What matters is that teens have the information they need to be protected physically and emotionally so they don't make dangerous choices based on faulty logic. There is advice on how to do this in the "real-world advice" section of each chapter. However, I can't recommend strongly enough that parents *not* corner their teenager and try to extract a confession. Making a teen feel like he can't talk about sex without being judged or attacked will make it far less likely that he'll ever bring up the topic again, even when he really needs help or advice.

Compelling as it may seem, sifting through a teen's e-mails or reading her diary are measures that should be used only in cases of true emergency. It's such a major invasion that if a parent gets caught (which is likely—teens have safeguards in place to fiercely guard their privacy), it can take a long time to rebuild that trust and credibility again—both of which are crucial to parents who want to guide their teens' choices.

TEENS ARE EXPLORING DANGEROUS TERRITORY, WITHOUT A MAP

Many teens tell me that they expect to sort through the questions, decisions, and issues concerning sex and sexuality alone. Some feel like they don't want to worry their parents. Others feel their parents have full plates and shouldn't be burdened with too much information. Still others don't want to disappoint their parents, don't want to invite too much inquiry into their personal lives, or simply assume their parents don't care to know.

Teens often tell me their belief that "what a parent doesn't know won't hurt them" is fostered by their parents' reaction whenever the teen does try to bring up a sensitive topic, especially sex. They tell me about parents who get angry or seem embarrassed or otherwise act in a way that makes the teen conclude this topic is off-limits. Something to note here is that teens will ascribe feelings to the adults in their lives that the adults themselves may not necessarily hold, based on things that are not said, tone of voice, or body language alone. So even if a parent is comfortable talking about sex with his or her teen but hasn't brought it up out of respect for the teen's privacy, the teen may assume that the parent doesn't want to talk about it, or that his parent would be angry or uncomfortable if the teen brought it up. And so the communication gap widens . . .

"I've always made a comparison between the way we treat driving and the way we treat sex," says Frank Furstenberg, Ph.D., professor of sociology at the University of Pennsylvania. What he means is: teens practice driving, often right in their parents' driveways. They get driving lessons. We know they want to drive, and we, in fact, expect they will drive, even though driving is a very dangerous activity—perhaps the most dangerous activity they will engage in while living with us. So we prepare them to drive, and we do everything we can to help them manage the risks associated with driving. On the contrary, says Furstenberg, parents expect sex *not* to happen ("knowing full well that it usually does") and distance themselves from the process of preparing teens to be sexually responsible.

When parents take an "I'd rather not know" approach, the result is not teens abstaining from sex. Teens won't wait while parents carefully construct the perfect thing to say or until it feels like it's just the right moment to talk. Instead, they forge ahead with their lives, which seem to have thousands of personal interactions an hour. Teens are exploring their sex and love lives on their own, without a map. And because many teens have gotten the message that their parents will be disappointed in them if they have sex or fool around, they are motivated to do what a person who doesn't want to disappoint someone they love does: they lie about it.

"Our parents think we won't lie to them"

"Things are never like parents see it at home. At home we are good, we don't cuss, and we do our chores like we're told. And in school, we listen to our teachers and walk with friends, like our parents think we do. But at school, we also cuss and ditch classes, and our parents don't even know about it until grades or reports go out. Then we lie and say they miscounted or something.

"Our parents think we won't lie to them to stay out of trouble. But we will. I've said I was at a girlfriend's house when I was really at the movies with a group of guy friends. Our parents grew up in the times that sex was for the people who were rebels. But now, I walk around school and see four or five girls who are pregnant. And we have a class where girls learn about being a mom.

"Although I choose to stay abstinent until after I'm married, like some others around here, we do wonder . . . and we have questions. Questions I'd get grounded for asking at home. And our questions are never answered. That's why I think a lot of teens go off and have sex. Because they are driven crazy about all the things in their heads, that they have to know."   —Francesca, 15, Arizona

So when parents bring up the topic of sex or fooling around, the teen looks away and mutters something about how they're not doing that kind of stuff—sure, other kids are doing it but they're not, so "Don't worry about it, Mom." To some parents, this is good news, not least because it so nicely fits into the parent's mind-set before this quickie conversation: "Phew. *Not my kid.*"

"NOT MY KID"

This brings me to the "not my kid" phenomenon. I considered calling this book *Not My Kid*, because time and time again I talk to parents who say that sure, they've heard about students who have sex at their teen's school and yes, they've heard about teens fooling around at parties but, thankfully, they were certain *their* teenager wasn't involved. Because I have teens in my life who I'm close to, and I'll admit it pains me to think about them fooling around, I understand where this desire to be in a little denial comes from. (See the introduction for my personal story about this.)

Denial that one's teenager is having sex is actually something of an epidemic in America. When a national study recently asked 14-year-olds "Are you having sex?" and then asked those same teens' parents "Is your child having sex?" only *one-third* of the parents whose teens were sexually active thought they were. The other two-thirds wrongly assumed their teens were virgins.

Still, less than half of high school students are sexually active, so taking a strictly odds perspective, it's more likely than not that the teen you care most about is a virgin. And even if that teen is sexually active, your feelings may range from "I guess it's okay as long as he is taking measures to protect against STDs and unwanted pregnancy and he's mature enough to handle a sexual relationship . . ." to "Well, this is worst-case scenario, but there's not much I can do about it." Either way, it's so hard to think about a child we love growing up in any way, and to think about them becoming sexually active may be the hardest change to grow accustomed to.

Parents Speak Out:
"She was so interested—and so young"

"What always kept me on edge is that my daughter (like many children, I suppose) was so interested, and at such a young age. And she always felt that she knew more than I did. Even at age 5, when I explained intercourse for the first time (her questions were very direct), she told me I was wrong. As she got older, and her sense of her right-ness and my wrong-ness became stronger, I was often concerned that she would avoid asking questions that might reveal that I knew something she didn't know, which could be embarrassing to her. Or I worried that she'd miss out on learning some important information because she thought she already knew it."

—New Jersey mother of an 18-year-old daughter

Most parents can remember feeling that, as a baby, their child was always one step ahead of them. Like when you put a baby in the "crawl position" and he takes off so easily that you're left wondering just how long ago he could have tried it. Now consider something that psychologist Jeanne Stanley (director of the Bryson Institute of the Attic Youth Center in Philadelphia) told me: "Most kids have already heard the term 'blow job' from other kids when they're nine. They maybe heard the word at eight but didn't know what it meant. By nine, they've heard it and they're starting to get more of an idea of what it is from their peers." Teens are still growing and still changing faster than we can imagine, and they are far more curious and probably more knowledgeable than most of us want to imagine. But anticipating what a teen will be thinking about a few months or even a few years down the line and broaching these topics with her ensures that she's well informed and that she has a source she can trust for honest answers to her questions. If you don't make an effort to stay a few steps ahead of her, however, she'll get the distinct impression that you're afraid to let her grow up, so why bother confiding in you at all?

"Our parents want us to stay babies forever"

"My parents want me to be a virgin until marriage, but in today's society that is just an impossibility. I am a girl who is about to turn 17, and amazingly I am still a virgin. Although that is about to change. I have a steady boyfriend who loves me, and we are having sex very soon. We have taken every precaution, we have protection and have both been tested for AIDS and other STDs—yay, we were both clean. Our parents believe that we are too young to be making this decision, but obviously we have thought this through and are being very safe about this.

"I think that parents just aren't ready for the fact that we are mature enough to make this decision. They want us to stay their little babies forever. But unfortunately, we do grow up, and they have to let go."   —Ann, 16, Maryland

Being in denial about a teen's current or future sex life at best makes the relationship more superficial than you'd probably like: consider that this is one of the most important issues to him, and you may be totally in the dark about his true feelings and actions. At worst, denial puts the teenager in danger; if he feels like it's not on your radar that he may be sexually active, he'll be less likely to come to you with questions, problems, or concerns about acting responsibly in this realm. And if he's sexually active and you don't know about it, he may not be getting the information he needs to protect himself both emotionally and from STDs and pregnancy—a risk no one can afford to take. This denial and the resulting communication gap, with teens afraid to talk to parents and parents feeling overwhelmed and unsure of how to talk to teens, contributes to three crises that threaten the welfare of our teenagers.

CRISIS I: TEEN PREGNANCY IS STILL A SIGNIFICANT PROBLEM

The United States still has the highest teen pregnancy rates in the industrialized world—more than 800,000 women under 20 become pregnant each year, and 80 percent of those pregnancies are unintended. And with how quickly youth culture changes, the positive trends we've been seeing could begin to reverse at any moment. "A new group of kids turns 13 every day, and we can't assume they'll make the same good choices their brothers and sisters increasingly are making," says Sarah Brown, director of The National Campaign to Prevent Teen Pregnancy.

Teens know teen pregnancy is an enormous problem. Many teens can even rattle off how many pregnant students are at their school (and how many pregnancy scares were suffered in the past month or two). Teens are motivated to resolve the issue of teen pregnancy—

even teens who are not sexually active view it as a very important issue—but they know they need help from parents and adults around them to do so.

CRISIS II: STDS ARE RAMPANT AMONG THE TEEN POPULATION

I speak often with researchers and health professionals, and many of them frequently complain to me that "Teenagers are not at all concerned about catching STDs." Why else, they wonder, would teens act the way they do? Teens don't use protection every time they have sex. Teens take their partner's word for it that they're "clean." Teens don't always see the doctor before they have sex, and they don't get tested frequently enough for diseases.

Though all these points may be true, I don't think these choices are a result of teens not caring. Sure, there is definitely a feeling of "I am invincible, and nothing bad will happen to me" among teens today (and teens of every year before them). But if you consider all the steps that need to be in place for teens to ward off STDs, many of them involve a good deal of adult communication and cooperation, as in driving to the doctor, paying for the office visit, and helping to sort through complex health information to make difficult decisions. Many teens tell me they are not getting this much-needed communication or cooperation from the adults in their lives, and the teens don't know how to ask for it. The result is too many teens with STDs that could have been avoided or treated earlier.

✳ How many young people have STDs? ✳

About 9 million teens and young adults
(ages 15 to 24) got an STD in the year 2000.
—CDC, 2004

"We like to say 'kids don't think it can happen to them,'" says Kathleen Ethier, Ph.D., a behavioral scientist in the division of STD prevention at the CDC. "But the truth is, *humans* don't like to think bad things can happen to them. We are overly optimistic. We underestimate the likelihood that anything bad will happen to us." And by proxy, we underestimate the likelihood that anything bad will happen to our teenagers, and we underestimate the steps we need to take to ensure their safety.

CRISIS III: IT IS EASIER THAN EVER FOR TEENAGERS
TO GET A SKEWED IDEA OF INTIMACY

It's sometimes easy to forget that teens are our next wave of adults, and increasingly the beliefs about love and sex that they learn as adolescents, beliefs that will set the stage for their adult behavior, are alarming.

When teens are surveyed about why they have sex, the reasons they give are often not the reasons that we, as adults, like to hear. Yes, there are definitely those teens who report that after prolonged discussions with their partner and trips to the doctor for both of them, the two procured birth control and STD prevention tactics and, as they were in a long-term and committed relationship, proceeded to initiate sexual relations. Far more common are the teens who say they felt pressured into having sex, either by their partner or by their friends.

Girls by the dozen tell me about their older boyfriends who made them feel mature, beautiful, exciting . . . and pressured them into having sex. (If a 13-year-old girl has a partner 6 years older, that couple is 6 times more likely to be having sex than a girl who's dating someone her own age.)

But even if the partner is not older, teens feel there's an expectation that sex will take place once you've been dating for a while, and the old "Once you say yes you can never say no again" myth is alive and well.

✳ Teens are feeling pressure to have sex ✳

27% of girls and 50% of boys age 15 to 17 "strongly agree" or "somewhat agree" that if you've been seeing someone for a while
"it is expected that you will have sex."
47% of girls and 56% of boys "strongly agree" or
"somewhat agree" that once you have had sex it is harder to say
no the next time.
—Kaiser Family Foundation, 2003

✳

34 percent of boys 15 and younger think it's okay for a boy to pressure
a girl to have sex if they have had sex before.
—National Campaign to Prevent Teen Pregnancy, 2003

One in ten girls age 15 and younger report that their first sexual experience was "involuntary," the definition of which involves a level of pressure bordering on coercion, a hazy gray area somewhere in between "a stranger grabbed me off the street" and "I did it but now I wish I hadn't." What follows is a classic story where sexual intimacy is coerced and the teenager is left knowing this experience went awry but not sure if she is to blame for the situation—or why she still has the feelings she does.

"He said: let's make a bet. If I win, you give me head."

"My boyfriend and I met at basketball camp. He is older, has a car, and a big tattoo—we are different. Three weeks into knowing him, one day we decide to go play soccer-tennis—a game we made up together—at a little park. So we get there and we'd been playing for a while and he says, 'Let's make a bet. If I win, you have to give me head.'

"A lot of guys say that and never mean it so I said 'Okay. It's a bet.' So we played and I lost. But it didn't matter to me, because I didn't think he was serious. Well then he asked, 'When do you want to do it?' And I told him I didn't care, it was up to him. So he said, 'Okay, right now.'

"By now I was scared. So I said, 'No, how about tomorrow.' Then he led me to his car. He says: 'Get in, it's okay, we'll just talk.' So, believing him, I got in. So I'm sitting there not knowing what to do or say and he says, 'Okay, give me head.'

"Now I know for sure he is serious, and I am terrified. I had never done anything like that before. The only thing I had done was make out. I keep coming up with lame excuses but he starts to get angry. He tells me if I don't do it in 5 minutes he's never going to talk to me again.

"Well, I couldn't bear him not talking to me. This, after all, is the guy I love. All the while I'm thinking to myself how this could ruin my reputation and how this isn't something that I do. Well by now he's very upset. So I get a little worried and I finally blurt out, 'Okay, I'll do it.' So I did it. After that we still hung out, but he would always ask me if I'd give him head again."   —Janice, 14, Oregon

Janice was clearly manipulated into a sexual situation, and many more teens tell me they feel pressure from their partner or their friends to have sex. It's a lose-lose for boys and girls, as boys may grow into men who pressure women to have sex and don't understand the hurt feelings and lack of intimacy that come afterward and girls may grow into women who think that this is what love and sex are supposed to feel like.

And though it's considered more acceptable and no longer generally thought of as embarrassing to be a virgin, both boys and girls are feeling pressure to start having sex in high schools across the nation, where a culture of "all the cool kids are doing it" still reigns.

"People think they are cool if they have sex"

"I am a regular teen guy, talking all the time and never when I am supposed to. My hobbies are soccer, and my favorite music is rap. I usually go to football games, friends' houses, go to the movies, ref soccer, and watch all the sporting activities on TV with my friends.

"Virginity is important to some people but not to others. I mean there are the 'bad-ass kids' and then there are the 'fun-to-hang-around' kids. The bad-ass kids don't really care, but the fun-to-hang-around kids do. Inside they know that no one in that group has done anything and won't do anything. People know that people are having sex because the kids come out and say it. They think that they are cool if they have sex, but most of the time it just makes them worse off later on in life.

"I have not been in love. Love is a powerful thing, and it is all talk. People say they love each other, but all they are saying is, 'I like you now but in 2 weeks you don't mean anything to me—you are just there.' They do not get their hearts broken—they just get it messed around with."   —Eli, 14, Missouri

As adults we may think of teens who have sex without taking steps to prevent STDs or pregnancy as being "reckless" or making "bad decisions." But often, having sex isn't a "decision" at all. Like some of the kids Eli refers to, too many teens report that sex isn't planned—that it "just happens." I asked 12- to-17-year-olds about this in the Tell the Truth! survey, and they confirmed that almost as often as not, sex is something that takes place with little or no fore-thought.

✻ Exclusive National Survey Results ✻
Teens: Tell the Truth!

Is sex usually something that people decide to do or
does it "just happen"?
Decide to do 41%
It just happens 34%
Don't know 25%

When sex "just happens" to teens, they are put at risk physically because they are not prepared to prevent STDs or unplanned pregnancy. They are also more vulnerable emotionally and susceptible to regret as feelings tend to evolve after sex. (I often hear from girls who thought that having sex would "bring the relationship to the next level of closeness" and are distraught to learn that their boyfriend doesn't feel the same way.)

Spontaneous sex occurs for many reasons which are discussed throughout this book, but one significant factor is that it's always more likely when drinking is involved. We know teens are having sex and fooling around while drunk, and a National Campaign to Prevent Teen Pregnancy study revealed that 17 percent of girls and 11 percent of boys 14 and younger agree that because of alcohol, they had been in a sexual situation that they later regretted.

"Alcohol and hormones do not mix well"

"Joe was my best male friend. You know, the one who would listen to anything. The one who I could call and talk to until the sun started to spread its rays through the window. I still miss that between us. As soon as I knew I was crazy about him I told him, but he shrugged it off.

'I'm not interested.' He told me at first. But a week after the initial telling he approached me about going on a date. Alcohol and hormones do not mix well, and I found this out the hard way. I was at Joe's house when we decided to slip back some shots of rum. After quite a few, I can't say I really remember, we ended up down in his basement, doing God knows what besides sex. The good thing about that night? I left there with a boyfriend."

—Greta, 17, New York

And then there's the much-debated issue of oral sex. There's not a lot of formal research on this topic, but a 2004 NBC/*People* poll showed that 12 percent of young teens (age 13 to 16) have had oral sex, and in 2003 a Kaiser study revealed that 36 percent of teens ages 15 to 17 (40 percent of males and 32 percent of females) had had oral sex. Of those teens, 24 percent said they had oral sex "to avoid having intercourse," which brings up an interesting point: many teens tell me that oral sex is considered an act that is less intimate than intercourse. It's a "base" (usually "third"). Teens talk about oral sex in a casual, almost flippant way. To wit: mid-tirade about how another girl stole her boyfriend, Julia, 18, from Chicago, told me, "And then I found out . . . that she gave him head on prom night!"

The end result of teens engaging in unwanted, unplanned for, or simply not-well-thought-out sex are teens who feel unhappy emotionally and are at risk physically, all of which could be avoided if there was not such a communication gap between teens and adults on this topic. There are, of course, teens who fool around or have sex who feel like they're ready, and others who sense that they are in over their heads but feel incapable of opting out. The compounding fear (or reality) of STDs and unwanted pregnancy risk keep teens off-balance. Many desire to have sex, because their bodies are telling them the time is right and after all, from what they've seen and heard, sex seems fun, adventurous, and gratifying. Yet at the same time, they understand that sex is a precarious proposition, a danger zone that can lead them to regret, or worse. Perhaps for all these reasons, the majority of teens, 66 percent, report regretting their first sexual experience.

But it doesn't have to be this way.

Since you're reading this book, on some level you suspect it's time to face this issue with the teen or teenagers you care about. Even though you know your teenager isn't a baby anymore, the thought of him or her becoming sexual may be one that you find particularly difficult to wrap your mind around. Just know that no matter what your values or beliefs, it behooves you greatly to know what's going on with your teenager and figure out ways to communicate effectively on this topic, because study after study confirms that you are in a position to have the most impact on your teenager's choices about sex.

REAL-WORLD ADVICE

In the face of the evidence about what teens' sex lives are like, it can feel overwhelming, like you are up against a force larger than yourself in your quest to keep your teen* safe from unwanted pregnancy, disease, and regrettable sexual experiences. "Pay attention to your own feelings," advises cognitive behavioral psychologist Robert Schachter, assistant clinical professor of psychology at Mount Sinai School of Medicine. "You're letting your baby grow up, and that's very difficult." Remember that less than half of teens are sexually active, and even in today's fast-paced, hyper-sexualized society, teens are showing signs of being more responsible in terms of contraception. Nonetheless, I realize your concern is not with "teens" in general but with your teen in particular, so let me give you the most important bit of information in this book: *you have far more power over the situation than you may know.* Here's how you can begin to use this power to help your teenager:

AVOID THE "NOT MY KID" TRAP

If you find yourself looking at these statistics and thinking, *Well sure, a percentage of teens may think/feel/act that way, but not my kid . . .* consider that even if 99 percent of teens act a certain way, if your teenager is the 1 who gets pregnant, contracts an STD, or has a regrettable sexual experience, then the statistics don't really matter at all. Even if you consider your teenager the ultimate example of a "good kid," you still need to be aware of her changing emotions and her need to discuss issues of sex and sexuality with you.

---

*Though this book is for parents, teachers, health educators, and everyone who cares about teens, the phrase "your teen" throughout refers to the teen or teens you personally are most concerned with.

Talk the Talk: Teenagers Will Listen if You Say...

"I read today that some teens lie about whether they are virgins to their friends. Why do you think people would do that?"

"What percentage of high school students do you think are sexually active? Yes, I thought it was that high, too. The truth is, less than half are sexually active. Do you think that's true for the teens at your school?"

REALIZE THAT, OF ALL THE INFLUENCES IN YOUR TEEN'S LIFE, YOU HAVE THE *MOST* INFLUENCE ON YOUR TEEN'S DECISIONS ABOUT SEX

Surprised? So were most parents. A 2004 National Campaign to Prevent Teen Pregnancy study asked parents who they thought had the most influence on their teen's decisions about sex. Almost half the parents guessed that their teen's *friends* had the most influence. In reality, 45 percent of teens (age 12 to 14) said *parents* were the most influential, then friends, who were a distant second at 31 percent.

"Peers do have a lot of influence," says Douglas Kirby, Ph.D., senior research scientist with ETR Associates, a California-based health education organization. "But parents can trump that." Kirby points out, "The more a young person is attached to their parents, the more important those values are." So if you have a tight relationship with your teen, there are ways (addressed in the "Real-World Advice" and "Talk the Talk" sections throughout this book) to help ensure that your values act as his or her main guide when making decisions about sex. If you don't have what you consider a close relationship with the teenager in your life, the advice and tips in this book will help you to get closer to your teen—just use the ones that feel comfortable to you until you develop more and more of a comfort level having these kinds of conversations. The first thing you can start to do is to ask your teen questions, not just about sex and who they're dating or interested in, but about their lives. The more open-ended questions you ask your teen, the more he or she will get comfortable opening up to you on all topics.

TIP: When talking with a teenager about sex, try to ask two questions for every statement you make. This will keep your conversation a dialogue.

USE NUMBERS TO START A CONVERSATION

Now you know the truth about who's doing what with whom and where, and to some extent, why. You can use these statistics as evidence to your teen that you know what's up. National Campaign to Prevent Teen Pregnancy polling data shows that teens overestimate how many other teens are sexually active, and when they find out the truth, teens say it's easier for them to abstain from sex now that they know *not* everyone is doing it.

Refrain, however, from using statistics as a weapon, as in, "Well, more than half of teenagers *aren't* doing it, so it turns out you actually *don't* know everything." This will just start an eye-rolling marathon. *Do* use them to start a dialogue.

DON'T BUY THE LIES

When you ask questions, your teen will give you answers. If this is kind of a new practice, your teen's first instinct may be to protect himself, which in many cases may include lying. Don't believe the lies teens tell you. They're not lying because they want to be believed; they're lying because they want you to challenge them. When they lie, and you believe them, a little bit of their faith and trust in you actually dies. This is hard to stomach because some teens are very good at lying. And because they often honestly believe they're lying "for your own good," it can be tough to catch them. But take it from me: teens *want* you to ask exactly where they're going and when they'll be home . . . and wasn't that homework due last week?

Questioning your teen if you suspect a lie is not fun. And telling your teen that you expect the truth from her is going to result in your getting some information that you may, deep in your heart, rather not know. Arguments will arise from this, and I'm sure it will be highly stressful while it's happening. I know this is sounding less and less like a good idea . . . but stay with me here.

Even though you are going to ask questions and get the truth, you are free from the burden of micromanaging your teen's life. You don't have to agonize over your teen's choices, because you don't get to make them for her. Your mission is to get the truth, give information, start a dialogue, and then allow your teenager the freedom to make her own decisions and create her own consequences. Ultimately, your teenager will see that giving you information will not result in your locking them in a high tower until they're 30 (right? you have to agree to that for all of this to work).

By getting in there with your teen—by making your relationship more sticky but also more truthful—you're keeping her from flying free into situations that she's not ready for, without the information she needs to be successful. You get all the glory of weighing in with your opinions and none of the pain of having to actually make the choice (though I know for some of us, shall we say, more controlling types, watching someone else make a choice is 10 times harder than making it yourself; but alas, that's the job description—I didn't write it, I'm just reporting it).

I can tell you that after the fighting dies down, teens whose parents catch them in lies, teens with parents who refuse to allow them to omit important information, teens whose parents make rules and enforce them—those teens speak proudly to me about their parents. They know their parents treasure them, and that gives them a lot of confidence. And that confidence, more often than not, translates into intelligent, "I am valued and valuable" decision making.

THE LAST WORD

A phrase I often notice teens using is some variation on "Parents see what they want to see." By this they mean that parents sometimes *say* they want to know what's really going on in their teen's sex life, but when the conversation gets uncomfortable, the parent bails out. As Ann (the 16-year-old who said she has a boyfriend and is planning to have sex soon) puts it: "I have tried to talk to my mother and she just says, 'Oh please tell me you are still a virgin . . . you are? Okay, good. Stay that way.' Parents will hear what they want to hear, and if they truly want us to be able to confide in them, they need to open up their ears, not judge us . . . and just *listen*."

The easy way out here is to play "Blame the Teen" so we don't have to feel responsible for the choices teens make, because after all, who can control teenagers? But this logic is faulty, and the sentiment is untrue and unfair to teens, who are looking to adults for guidance that they know they desperately need in this area—even if they don't want to admit it. By picking up this book and committing to finding out the truth about teens and sex, you have made yourself someone who wants to listen, who wants to see what lies between the hyped-up stories in the press and your teen's reticence: what's *really* going on with teens and sex today. Listening to teens tell you about their sex lives and what their true thoughts are on this important topic is a rare chance to get a behind-the-scenes look at a formative part of teens' existence and an exciting opportunity to use that information to help the teen or teens you care about most act smart—and stay safe.

Some of the **Hype** About Teens and Sex Is True . . . and Some Is Just Hype

✳ **Exclusive National Survey Results** ✳
Teens: Tell the Truth!

Of 12-to 17-year-olds surveyed:

✳

1 in 10 agree:
"It's considered normal for someone my age to have sex with someone they met at a party."

✳

1 in 7 agree:
"It's considered normal for someone my age to have sex with a new boyfriend or girlfriend."

✳

1 in 3 agree:
"It's considered normal for someone my age to have sex with a long-term boyfriend or girlfriend."

✳

48% agree:
"It's not normal for people my age to have sex."

I hear stories about what teens are up to in a fairly predictable pattern: one or two will mention something that sounds familiar (usually couched with the modifier "you know"). Next, there's a word or catchphrase that everyone starts using to describe it (like "chicken parties"). Then everyone's talking about it, which means probably 0.5 to 5 percent of teens are actually doing it. Once in a while, it means that just one group of kids did it, but it was such a good story that it got forwarded around to a bunch of e-mail address books until it took on the vibe of a national trend—like a quickie suburban legend.

At this point, the trend either dies (meaning it may get reported in the adult press but teens have moved on to something else) or it gets picked up by the masses, oftentimes as a less-radical version of the original trend. So if the gossip is about "rainbow parties" (where girls all wear different colored lipsticks and each makes a different ring on the same guy's penis), as a mainstream trend this might evolve into more girls trying oral sex (even at parties) because it's been a bit more normalized after they've heard about it over and over.

Again, this is my experience as someone who communicates regularly with teens across the country. We will likely never see federal research money devoted to studying why some girls suddenly start wearing colored bracelets that reportedly indicate how far they've gone sexually, or why, two months later, we keep hearing about a game called "Snap," where if a boy breaks said bracelet off a girl she is "required" to perform said act with him. (Again, how many teens actually did this? I know a lot more teens who talk about the bracelets and what they meant than would actually admit to wearing them as symbols or "playing" Snap.)

Teens are complex and often contradictory. Even within one single high school, there can be 20 or more cliques, plus dozens of kids who don't feel they fit into any one clique, and even within cliques, each teen has his or her own individual sets of values and mores. That said, there are some trends that reveal how teens are thinking, feeling and talking about sex and sexuality in general. You'll notice that these trends themselves are contradictory, in that various opposing trends are affecting different subsets of the teen population at the exact same time. It'll be interesting to see how they play out over the next few years. You can, of course, influence how they play out with your teen by discussing them. Unlike the statistics in Chapter 1, these trends do not reflect the ways most teens are acting, but rather, the way some teens are trending, which means others may follow.

TREND #1: TEEN SEX IS MORE CASUAL

There has been a lot of press about how busy teens are and how this overscheduling and pressure is leading to the "friends with benefits" (FWB) phenomenon, where teens get together to fool around (or have sex) but skip the relationship part. The idea of "friends with benefits" is not a new one—the expression was also popular in the 1990s. Back then, FWB generally meant teens were fooling around with someone who was not a boyfriend or girlfriend, but who was probably in their circle of friends. The newer definition of FWB has expanded to mean having a sexual relationship with someone a teen may be tangentially friends with—it's more like friends of friends with benefits.

✳ How many seniors have FWB? ✳

About 40% of 12th graders have had sex outside of a romantic relationship.
—National Institute of Child Health and Human Development, 2004

When you talk to teens about FWB, scratching below the surface you'll find right away that the old double standard is alive and well. Girls will generally say FWB is bad for girls, who can get stuck with a bad reputation if they fool around too much, and good for boys, whose reps are enhanced when they fool around. As a result, girls, especially younger girls, often tell me they think the whole FWB concept is pretty flawed.

"A friend with benefits is the most stupid thing"

"A 'friend with benefits' is the most stupid thing on this planet. At my school that means: *I have a man, you got a girl, but hey, we are just friends that have sex.* That's like saying *we are married, but since you are my husband's friend with benefits, both of us will just have sex with him.* That's so gross!"   —Candice, 14, South Carolina

Though it's frequently put forth as a rationalization for FWB, the notion that teens are overprogrammed and have become "too busy to date" so they are resorting to hooking up sans romance is not supported, anecdotally, by teens. It's not that teens are too busy to date (if you've ever watched a teen engage in a five-way text-messaging marathon that goes on for 20 minutes, you know teens make time for things they really want to do). It's more that developing one-on-one romantic relationships has not necessarily been set for them as a goal or a value, especially not in high school. We no longer expect (or even want) teens to fall in love with the person they might marry while they're still in high school. At the same time, teens are bombarded by sexual messages from pop culture and the media to add to their already revved-up hormones, coupled with a very strong "don't have sex" message from parents and educators. It's this confluence of messages that seem to add up to the trend (and again, this is the minority) of teens who are hooking up sexually outside of a romantic relationship. To some teens, sex and fooling around, ironically, seems less wrong when it's not surrounded by a big, heavy relationship . . . when it's not made into such a big deal.

And yet, teens (like adults) are driven to connect with each other. They want to have relationships and be intimate. Girls in particular long to be in love. So what happens when "hooking up"—fooling around casually—becomes an expectation in a given clique or high school is that the behavior is normalized, but the emotions that go along with the behavior do not evolve quite as quickly. In other words, many girls who fool around casually are, in their hearts, hoping the relationship will evolve into love, while for boys, the relationship between fooling around and love is completely different. It's not that the guys are taking advantage of the girls; it's more like they don't fully understand what the girls are expecting. To a guy, the situation presents as, "this girl is willing to fool around with me"—and what guy wouldn't find that prospect appealing? This miscommunication is fostered by girls who may even be telling the guys that they're just interested in a casual hook-up, even if in their hearts it's not true. Because a girl knows that seeming into a hookup will appeal to a guy, she may figure, well, some "love" from him is better than no attention from him at all.

This same dynamic plays a role in the evolution of how teens think about and engage in oral sex. It used to be thought of as very intimate, an act that would occur after intercourse, and only in very close and trusting relationships. Now oral sex is thought of by some teens as being far less intimate than intercourse. "I've gone to third—meaning oral—with this guy and we've only been going out for about 4 months," says Sandy, 14, from Illinois "We're thinking about having sex, but I don't know if I'm ready yet . . ." Despite the fact that many STDs can in fact be transmitted via oral sex, oral sex is also thought of by teens as "risk-free" sex. In truth, I've never heard from a single teen who admitted to using condoms during oral sex.

Although there isn't a lot of trending data about how many teens are having oral sex and how young they are starting to do it (in part because researchers are loathe to ask young teens or preteens if they are having oral sex), a 2003 Kaiser study showed that 36 percent of 15- to 17-year-olds have engaged in oral sex.

There is also a smattering of talk about anal sex as a pregnancy-free alternative to vaginal intercourse, though my impression is there's more talk than action on this trend.

And again, echoing the belief that teens today have a different barometer for what is intimate, I am hearing more about sex play in public or semi-public forums—teenagers fooling around at parties, on buses, even in school auditoriums.

"People were on top of each other . . . groping and making out"

"One of my best friends is a girl and she lets me in on all the dirt, and I cannot believe what I am hearing. She tells me boys at parties are fingering girls and girls are letting them. One time at a party I was at there was a trampoline in the back and it started off as being something fun that we kind of jumped on and wrestled, but as the night went on we looked back on that trampoline because a lot of people were missing and they were out there on top of each other groping each other and making out. The girl that threw the party was not involved in any of this so you can imagine how pissed she was . . ."
—Larry, 14, Colorado

It's important to consider, when hearing about teens-and-sex trends, that sex is such a part of our culture and so talked about in pop culture that teens are fairly comfortable talking about sex with each other, with new "friends" on the Internet, with acquaintances at school. So this can give the image that more fooling around is going on than is really taking place. In other words, a lot of the talk—particularly the talk about sex games teens play, like with the bracelets or "who can score the most girls/guys" kinds of games—is more about the talk than the action.

"If you go all the way, you win"

"The girls and the guys around here wear gel bracelets. It stands for not being afraid to mess around with a guy or girl. We have a game that we play at our school called 'nervous.' It's where you go as far as you can go with a guy or a girl, without getting nervous. If you go all the way you win . . . and if you admit that you're nervous you lose."
—Nora, 14, Texas

Some teens, however, particularly teens who are more easily influenced, are vulnerable to believing that fooling around is carefree fun—and it is only after the fact that they may (or may not) experience negative outcomes in the form of regret or other undesirable consequences. Sex is an attractive proposition, and one that teenagers are eager to justify. If a teenager has even one friend who engages in oral sex or intercourse and doesn't act like they regret it, and that friend doesn't seem to have any STDs, then it seems like, "What's the big hoopla about this anyway?"

✳ Exclusive National Survey Results ✳ Teens: Tell the Truth!

At your school, sex is considered:

Pretty casual 39%

Fairly serious 27%

Very intimate 7%

Don't know 27%

Yet as any adult knows, fooling around for the sake of it, or for the wrong reasons, can bring regret and heartbreak to both girls and guys. "There are guys who feel an enormous amount of pressure to fool around," says Elizabeth Casparian, Ph.D., who is director of educational programs at HiTOPS, a teen health clinic and education center in Princeton, New Jersey. "They can't admit to their friends that they didn't enjoy it or that they felt bad after; it's hard for them to admit it to themselves. But it happens all the time."

Remember that many teenagers are making decisions based on their research set of one-to-five other teens, and those teens' description of the experience is going to be a pretty compelling picture. This is why it's so important not to exaggerate or make sweeping negative statements about sex. If someone in your teen's day-to-day life has the opposite experience, your credibility can be dashed by some precocious 14-year-old's salacious description of sex, be it real or imagined.

"There's a lot of sexual intimacy"

"I have a friend who goes out a lot, and he tells me about all these girls he meets and later on he always ends up in trouble cause there's a lot of girls sleeping around. It's hard to find decent girls. He's still a virgin, but he does making out: just sitting on a couch and having very long kissing sessions. Probably feeling up on her. Guys do sleep around, but I mean, just teenagers in general. There's a lot of sexual intimacy; I think it's dumb. There's no need to, really. And definitely there are a lot of teen pregnancies and STDs."

—Ethan, 16, California

Yet there are teens, like Ethan (and Peter, below) who seem to understand that fooling around, with or without intercourse, carries with it the twin-baggage set of intimacy and responsibility.

"Virginity isn't important at my school— just to me"

"I go a public school that has about 1,000 kids for each grade level. People are hooking up all over the place. I mean, people hookup all the time, wherever they can. People hookup more at their houses compared to anywhere else, but people still hookup in school, movies, the malls and football games.

"I haven't had too many girlfriends—I don't see a purpose in dating someone just for kicks. Virginity isn't that important at my school, it's just important for me. That would be another reason for me not having many girlfriends. A lot of people are having sex, and everyone seems to hear about it. My friends are very much like me. I talk to my parents about my relationships, but don't go too in depth about it. It ends up all the rumors you hear about sex are true, at least at this school."

—Peter, 15, Pennsylvania

Still, it's easy to see how guys (and girls) might feel like they are "supposed" to be having sex.

I listened when my parents said:

"Save yourself until you find someone who truly loves you for you."

—Boy,* 17, Mississippi

TREND #1, PART II: TEEN SEX IS *LESS* CASUAL . . .

Statistics show that teens on the whole are having less sex and using more contraception—these teens have even been labeled "the Cautious Generation" by more than one article and survey. On the leading edge of this movement are a number of formalized abstinence movements that are influencing some subsets of teen culture. I even hear buzz about "purity balls": father-daughter formal dances that take the place of prom.

As you surely know, there's been an influx of government funding for abstinence-only education (more about this in Chapter 6) and comprehensive sex ed. also stresses abstinence as a first line of defense against unwanted pregnancy and STDs. These classes may be having an impact on teens' choices.

When teens are surveyed, they often say that religious or moral beliefs play some role in their decision to remain virgins, and this was supported by the teens I spoke to as well.

"Most girls I know lose their virginity fairly young: 13, 14, 15, and 16," says Jill, 14, from Arizona. "But I am a virgin and I plan to stay that way until I'm married. I see my friends getting so hurt and regretting that they lost something so special. I also believe my

---

*All of the "I listened when my parents said" quotes are gleaned from the Teens Tell the Truth! survey. To protect these teens' privacy, I was only told their age, gender, and home state, which is how they will be identified throughout this book.

body isn't my own; it belongs to God, and I should stay true to my future spouse."

Teens are also telling me about new and different kinds of virginity pledges that involve special rings or pendants that parents give their teens, sometimes as a part of an elaborate ceremony, which may feel more weighty than having them sign a card at an after-school activity.

Nearly all the teen virgins I communicated with mentioned that staying a virgin was a challenge—a worthwhile challenge, but by no means an easy one.

"It's harder than I thought it would be"

"I live in the city where sex is a very big part of everyday life. I can honestly say people are shocked to hear me declare my virginity so proudly. I think it was when I turned 17 that I realized it would be harder than I thought. I started to date and got feelings I had never had before. I even came close to having sex once . . . but I realized that it wasn't a person I wanted to have my first experience with."

—Valerie, 18, Pennsylvania

Voices such as Valerie's reinforce the idea that there's a lot more than "just say no" to helping a teen retain virginity through high school.

There has also been a bit of a backlash among some teens (particularly younger teens) who feel that sex is being shoved at them by movies, music, and TV, and they resent it. "There's a lot of movies and TV shows that would be perfectly fine without all the sex," said one teenage guy. And another 13-year-old girl watched a video of a famous pop star with me. When I noticed her looking away as the singer gyrated, she asked me, "Why does she have to do that part? It's gross." Those two teens were virgins, and many of the teens who feel this way tell me they don't feel ready for sex and dispute the implication that they somehow should be. The rise in high-school virginity may be, in part, reflecting this sentiment.

"I've never had a girlfriend, and I feel fine"

"A lot of people feel like they need to have a girlfriend 'cause they're so used to having one. But I've never had a girlfriend before, and I feel fine.

"I'd have to say our parents aren't really active in our lives. I definitely wouldn't go to my parents to talk about sex. Because I don't really feel comfortable talking with my parents just in general. We don't really talk much. It doesn't really concern me because I'm going to wait until marriage to have sex.

"People talk about love, but I don't think you find love in high school. High school is just your teenage years, learning, having fun, I never really think of it as a time for love."   —Ethan, 16, California

A lot of teens echoed this statement, that high school isn't really a time for love. But I also heard from teens who were very much in love and planned on staying with their boyfriend or girlfriend for a long time. It seems to be a minority of teens, though, who feel that they'll find true love in high school.

Teens' mixed feelings about love and its place in their sex life are exemplified by one particular statistic from the Truth survey:

✳ Exclusive National Survey Results ✳
Teens: Tell the Truth!

Sex should be romantic

True 78%

False 3%

Don't know 19%

It's nice, but not too surprising that 78 percent of 12- to 17-year-olds think sex should be romantic. But it's fascinating, and perhaps most telling of all, that 19 percent of teens "don't know" if sex should be romantic or not. Teens are conflicted about just how serious, romantic, and generally how big a deal sex is supposed to be.

TIP: To see what kinds of discussions teens are having about sex right now, check out some smaller, more personal sites like scarleteen.com or purplepjs.com as well as "Teens Tell All" on teenpregnancy.org.

TREND #2: GIRLS WANT HOOKUPS (NOT RELATIONSHIPS)

This is a trend that gets a lot of press, perhaps because many people find it such a titillating idea: that girls are just as interested as guys in the no-strings-attached hookup. Though there are some girls and guys who subscribe to this idea, from my research, it's far less common than you may believe. What I do hear a lot of, however, are guys who feel pressured to have sex or fool around. Though most of that pressure comes from friends or, on occasion, their dads, there is an occasional guy, like this one, who feels that girls expect him to go too far, too fast:

"After 2 months of dating, she was wanting to get intimate"

"I'm 16, and have a lot of friends, but only a few true friends. Anyway, back in November, I met a girl. I really liked her and she really liked me. But she was different than me, she liked to party, drink, drive fast, all this stuff that I didn't do. I asked her out, and we started going out, like girlfriend and boyfriend.

"We got close though, really quick. After about 2½ months of dating, she was wanting to get intimate. I'll never forget when she asked me this one question: 'When do you think we'll start having sex?' I was shocked. I mean, come on, after two months of going out? I let it go, but that next week she asked me if I wanted to come over, she said her parents were going over to a neighbor's house for the night.

"She did say, 'If you don't want to do anything you don't have to,' but the pressure is already there. I try to have morals and not do stuff with girls whenever I want. Even when it is really tempting. All my friends have these girls, and they're 'friends with benefits,' that's fine and everything, but it goes a lot farther than most people think. 'Friends with benefits' is just another way of saying, *I don't like you, but I think you're hot and want to do stuff with you*—like oral sex. Me, I like going to the movies and kissing and cuddling, but I know girls and guys who have gone to the movies and gone below the belt. I can't do that stuff with girls, I mean I really want to, but I can't . . . I feel bad about it if I do."   —Craig, 16, Oklahoma

Generally speaking, this type of pressure occurs when the girl is older than her boyfriend. True, there is a bit of a movement on the part of some girls to rebel against the stereotype that girls want love and guys want sex. But this does not commonly take the form of girls finding it fun and empowering to give group blowjobs at a party or competing for who can have sex with the most guys. Yes, it does happen, and it would be easy to find a teenager to testify that this is happening in their school. But again, it is my sense that this falls into the category of talk rather than action. And when it does happen, I'm not convinced it's the girls who are initiating it, and even if they *do* initiate this kind of activity, based on my talks with girls, casual fooling around does not make teen girls feel empowered before, during, or after the fact.

It's true that some girls like to dress in sexy clothes, perhaps because they are experimenting with feeling sexy and showing the world that they are desirable. Or sometimes it's because they're comfortable with their bodies and excited about how they look and they're confident enough to show it off. I want to warn against making assumptions about how any teens feel or act based on what they wear. Many observers have based their "girls want to fool around with no strings attached" theories on the fact that they look around and see teen girls who may appear as if they want to do just that. But just because a girl wears her thong sticking out of her pants or even dons a Playboy pendant or other suggestive clothes or trinkets does not mean she is having sex or even fooling around.

It is, however, important to talk to girls about what kind of message their clothes are sending to guys and men, who may not appreciate the nuance of what's fashionable now and instead view suggestive clothes as just that: suggestions that the girls are ready to be sexual. On the flip side, it is worth telling boys that girls who dress in sexy clothes may do so for a variety of reasons and not to read into their wardrobe and assume that they want to have sex.

TREND #2, PART II: GIRLS WANT RELATIONSHIPS (NOT RANDOM HOOKUPS)

This is nothing new, actually, the idea that girls are looking for a committed relationship, while guys are looking for free sex. Girls are influenced by the reputation factor. Having a boyfriend is better than not having a boyfriend, and fooling around too much or too publicly (or sometimes, even at all) can still get you branded a "slut" (guys still have that get-out-of-bad-rep-free card).

"I have to settle for guys who just want a hookup"

"Dating in my hometown is always a big deal—or actually, hooking up is. It's like a big line of drama that people just like to build up and tell everyone about. At my school, people are always talking about who hooked up with who the night before or whatever.

"I can't get a guy who just wants a relationship. When I want that, I have to settle for the guys who just want a hookup like making out or doing other stuff. But I get so many guys who just want hookups (because they find out what I did with a guy) that I can't get rid of them.

"I only want a guy for a relationship, but most of the guys out there are just in it for the hookup, like having sex and giving head. Girls always get drawn into that phase where they think the guy really cares about them because he spends so much time with them or they get told sweet things that they think mean something. Guys tell girls things they want to hear, to convince the girls to do it or they will stick around for a while to get more . . . and then just drop the girls when they are done with them—done getting what they want."

—Giselle, 15, Florida

Many girls tell me that they feel that much of the random hooking up, on the part of girls, is not really an expression of a take-charge, sexually free mind-set. It's just as likely to be a misguided effort on the girl's part to get a guy to like her. Other girls and guys say girls are in a position now where some feel like they're supposed to want to have oral sex or they're supposed to want to fool around, so they get in situations in which they don't know how to handle themselves and they get swept along into hooking up or having oral sex.

TREND #3: TEENS' LIVES (AND SEX LIVES) ARE *MORE* PRIVATE

With virtually all teenagers online, e-mailing and IM-ing each other, and text-messaging on their cell phones, parents have been cut out of the loop for a great majority of teen conversations. Gone are the days when guys had to call the house to get a girl on the phone, when even if the parent didn't answer the phone and screen the call, they at least heard the phone ring and could ask the teen who was on the line. With teens dating more as a group activity and less one-on-one, there's less "I'll pick you up at your house"—and, therefore, less opportunity for parents to check out a date.

This may account, in part, for teens' often claiming that their parents "don't have a clue" what they're up to. Teens' privacy also puts a huge burden on the teens, because it's so easy to keep things from their parents, teens feel like they should be able to handle many adult decisions by themselves. In fact, many teens expressed to me that parents should just "not worry," that they've "got it covered." Unfortunately, many of those same teens went on to tell me about the decisions they were making, often with little knowledge or faulty logic in place.

"There's not a lot my parents can do to stop me"

"Drinking and doing drugs play a huge role when hooking up. Many of my friends lost their virginity while drunk or high. You are more likely to say yes, or just not care, when you are drunk or high. I myself was sexually assaulted when I was drunk once. I couldn't stop him or say no, because I was so drunk. Luckily, someone stopped it and I was not raped.

"Parents cannot do a whole lot to stop their kids from doing these things. I have been caught drinking and punished for months and I still go out and drink and smoke. Now when my parents start to say 'Were you out drinking? What are you guys going to do? I don't know if we like this situation . . .' I just say, 'Mom, Dad, I would never do anything to lose your trust again. I am trying to make up for past mistakes and would never do anything to ruin the faith that you have in me. I'm sorry for what I did, and I never want to be in trouble like that again.' Then they let me go out and I have a good time, drinking, smoking, and whatever else my heart desires. Parents will see what they want to see. Mine think I am sorry and will never do it again. Well, drinking and smoking are my decisions. They can talk to me about it till they are blue in the face, but in the end it is my decision to drink or do drugs and they would have to lock me in my room at all hours to stop me. Well, actually I have alcohol in my room so even that couldn't stop me.

"It is not like I'm not a good kid. I get good grades and got high scores on my SATs, and I play on sports teams, too. I work hard so I like to play hard and have fun.

"Parents, we are going to make our own decisions and make our own mistakes. Sometimes you just have to let go and let us or else we just might rebel harder against you."   —Elmira, 16, Iowa

It takes far more effort in this information age to figure out who a teen's friends are, where she is after school (since she can call you from anywhere on her cell), and who she's with. However, now more than ever, it's so important to commit to doing just that.

Not all teens, but many teens feel comfortable lying to their parents. They sometimes even feel like they're lying "for their parents' own good." "Why worry my parents," they figure, "when this is a situation that I can handle on my own?" This feeling is most often voiced by teens who report that their parents are very strict and have a blanket policy of saying no to "everything."

"We are getting married—secretly"

"My boyfriend and I had only been dating three months when he popped the question. I really don't know what went through our minds when he asked me. I said yes. Well we haven't told our parents yet and it has been two months since then. When he comes down here we are getting married secretly! I haven't told my mom and I want to. I don't know how or what to tell her. I am afraid she will be mad and upset with me. I am 18 and he is a little older. I am worried about what to do.

"My boyfriend is starting to get a little aggressive and bossy. I am starting to have second thoughts. I have had feelings come and go that he is cheating, though he says he isn't. I am still working things out in my mind. Life is so hard. I am really torn thinking about this . . ."   —Leila, 18, Tennessee

What the two previous teens have in common is that they're both making what seem like bad choices, one with mock bravado and one with a good deal of trepidation. The second teen feels like she could use guidance from her parents but is afraid to ask; the first teen feels like she doesn't need any help but clearly does. Both of these girls would benefit greatly from continuous and honest talks with their parents about sex and relationships. They epitomize why one talk is never enough.

TREND #3, PART II: TEENS' LIVES (AND SEX LIVES) ARE *LESS* PRIVATE

The same technology that keeps parents out of the loop also gives them a direct line into teens' innermost thoughts. Anyone can go to livejournal.com or teenopendiary.com (there are many more; search for "teen diary" to get more options) and check out teens' no-holds-barred online diaries. Read 10 or 20 different teen entries, and see what teens are up to, thinking, and feeling on all issues, including romance and sex. Go to sites with message boards where teens congregate, and you can "listen in" on their conversations. There is actually unprecedented access to teens' innermost thoughts and feelings, if you know where to look. This kind of research can also offer a great jumping-off point for discussions ("I read the most interesting thing today online, it was written by another 16-year-old. She said . . .").

There's also a dark side to the ease with which teens can share information with each other. In 2004, a city magazine reported a story in which a teen girl from a tony private school videotaped herself engaged in an intimate act and e-mailed it to a guy she liked. He then posted the film on the Internet for all his friends to see. And rumors, true or not, can have a much more intense and horrible impact on someone's reputation and self-esteem when they're sent through e-mail to tens, hundreds, even thousands of students at once.

Teens' increasing comfort level with expressing sexuality is not limited to online chatter. In May 2004, a California paper, the *Fresno Bee*, reported that schools were being forced to cancel dances because of the proliferation of freak-dancing—dancing that simulates sex moves, including "doggy-style" dancing and horizontal, pelvic-thrusting dance moves. One girl was quoted as saying that girls were giving boys lap dances at their homecoming dance. And at schools from California to Maryland, principals are banning certain dance moves and videotaping dancing with the threat that anything too bawdy will be played for the teens' parents.

Then there are the reports of teens fooling around at parties or on buses—the issue that generated the whole idea for this book. If you ask around, you will likely find stories from other parents about teens fooling around at parties, on field trips, even during assemblies at school. How rampant this trend has become is unclear, but the way teens are talking about it points to the fact that it's really happening (and is not just a good story to pass around). Enough of them have stories about it that are so varied and specific that they ring true.

✳ Exclusive National Survey Results ✳
Teens: Tell the Truth!

Of 12- to 17-year-olds surveyed:
1 in 11 say they have been in a situation where people were having
sex in front of other people.

Why are some teens fooling around more publicly? In part it's the purest form of pack mentality: if those kids over there are doing it, it must be okay. Any reservations someone has about fooling around may be quelled if they can actually see sex happening with little obvious ill effect. And, of course, alcohol almost always plays a role in these kinds of sex games, making teens feel more invincible and more vulnerable to suggestion.

Parents Speak Out: "The kids do it on the bus"

"The kids are doing each other on the buses. A party planner in my town said they need chaperones because they know what goes on in the buses, so I volunteered. We wouldn't let them do anything to one another. The kids tried to get rid of us. They said 'All the other chaperones stay in the front. We don't like you back here. You make us nervous.' Both the boys and the girls were vocal about it.

"I was very disappointed because I've been teaching kids for a long time—thirty years. When my kids went to school, in the '80s, it wasn't like that. It wasn't blatant, it wasn't out in the open; it was private. You would think the kids from this area would not be the faster crowd, historically. They don't grow up on the streets. They're not as quick to grow up . . . or so you would think."

—Chicago mother of two grown sons

Teens who fool around in groups or have multiple sex partners are exposing themselves to dangers, not least of which is the groupings of STDs such as gonorrhea of the throat that health officials are noting in various communities. Robin Stein, director of the Chicago-area teen health and education center Response Center, told me a story about a small town in her area where a large group of seventh- and eighth-grade students ("almost the whole class") were getting tested for chlamydia and oral herpes. "They had been doing that buddy sex with all these guys in their class," Stein says, "and there were about 40 kids who ended up infected with STDs—so that was kind of an eye-opener."

I heard stories like this one from health professionals and parents all over the country. "There's a lot of sharing of partners," says Michaeline Rittenman, a nurse practitioner at a Planned Parenthood in upstate New York. "All of a sudden we'll see groups coming in for STD testing, and they all seem to know each other." This trend is particularly upsetting when you consider another theme health professionals are constantly lamenting: teens seem unconcerned about STDs. "They feel it's not going to happen to them," says Rosemary Prentice, a family nurse practitioner who is on the faculty of the University of Southern Maine. "And if it does, they feel STDs aren't a big deal anyway. So then when you have to tell them: you have genital warts, or: you have HPV, which can lead to cervical cancer . . . that's a lot for somebody who's not been sexually active for a long time to deal with."

In addition to the health hazards, when teens look around and not just think everyone is doing it but *see* that everyone actually *is* doing it, it's easy for some to feel after the fact that they got swept along into fooling around, that the sex "just happened." That can bring feelings of regret, especially if their behavior at a party in retrospect, went against their morals or beliefs.

REAL-WORLD ADVICE

No matter how many scary articles you read or stories you hear about teens engaging in risky sexual activities, it never fails to be shocking and intriguing. That's why we keep reading about them: "teen sex" sells. Many times, when I spoke to experts in the course of writing this book, before I'd even ask a question, they'd say, "Please don't ask me to go on and on about the 'oral sex epidemic.' It's just not justifiable."

So even though you're reading here about some trends that may in fact be occurring at your teen's school, the intention is not to alarm you or to say that this is what the teens you know are definitely up to. But remember how trends tend to spread; even if they do become a weaker version of themselves, they still have impact. Most people would agree that it's not a good idea for teens to have sex at a party— or to have unprotected sex under any circumstances. Aside from the physical dangers, there can be dramatic emotional consequences.

We can't protect teens from wanting to experiment, and we can't keep them home from every single dance, party, or group outing that sounds suspect. We can, however, arm them with the good judgment they need to handle whatever situation they encounter with confidence and care.

LET THE NEWS INSPIRE CONVERSATION

Next time you see a study or an article about teens and sex, bring it up with your teenager. You can say, "You know, I read in the paper that teens are wearing these gel bracelets—is that going on in your school? Have you ever heard about that kind of a 'game'? What do you think about it?" You're not judging those teens who do engage in certain trends (because if it turns out your teen is involved, you don't want him to clam up), but you're showing your teenager that you don't just blindly accept the stories you read about his life; you want to hear what's going on straight from him.

REMIND YOUR TEEN TO BE IN CONTROL

If you've ever tried to talk your teen into anything, you know that they want, more than anything, to make her own decisions. Make it clear to your teenager that you value her judgment, so much so that you always want her to be in control, because you trust her far more than you trust some other teen you don't know (and even more than the teens you do know). That's why you want her to remember: she's in control. Her decisions are hers alone to make. So if there's ever an opportunity to either take control or cede it, you expect her to take it.

REMEMBER: YOUR TEEN IS WATCHING YOU

What you say is important, but how you act is also a powerful indication of your expectations as far as your teenager is concerned. "Even if they fake disinterest, you'd better believe that they are watching," says Michael Resnick, Ph.D., professor of pediatrics and director of the Healthy Youth Development Prevention Research Center at the University of Minnesota School of Medicine.

Parents Speak Out:
"It's about how you are, day to day"

"I've come to the conclusion, after talking to many parents and seeing kids who have gone down a different path—a dangerous one—that it has less to do with how puritanical your ethics are—it really is how you live your day-to-day life and how true and honest you are in your daily habits. Kids from extra tightly gripped parents don't necessarily turn out better. I don't think forbidding and denying works. Let your kids know how you feel on a day-to-day basis in a natural way. Take opportunities, like when you hear a rumor, to find out their opinion . . . rather than preaching at them."

—Nevada mother of three teen boys

Talk the Talk: Teenagers Will Listen if You Say...

"You know we talk a lot about making smart decisions, and you know I trust your judgment. That's why I prefer that you be in control, in almost any situation. Like if people are drinking at a party, I would trust you to be the designated driver and not to rely on someone else not to drink, because I trust you more than I trust those other kids. And sexually speaking, I want you to be the one to make decisions about how far you'll go, and when and where and with whom. I don't trust some guy [or girl] to make that decision for you. Listen, at the end of the day, the only person who has to live with your choices is you. Better you make them knowing you were in control than later to feel like decisions were made for you.

"Have you ever felt like you gave up control of a decision or were being pressured to? Even which movie to go to or where to go for dinner? It's normal to sometimes give up what you want to make your friends happy, but I can tell you that I knew some girls [or guys] who felt decisions about sex were made for them, and that is not a good feeling. And listen, people who want to justify what they're doing will always try to get more people to join them. So if you're ever in a situation where people around you are doing something that makes you feel even a little uncomfortable, I hope you'll make your own decision about it. You can always call me if you want to leave."

Let your teenager see you struggle with hard decisions, stand up for yourself when things seem wrong, and make choices that are difficult but right. It's hard to fathom sometimes because teenagers can seem more like young adults than like children, but even though they're not little kids anymore, teens continue to look to you as an example.

THE LAST WORD

By having these conversations with your teen, you're showing her that her decisions impact her twice—once in the moment and again as both the memory and ramifications of that decision take hold. A good way to reinforce this is to say that you always want her to think about decisions in terms of how she'll feel about the outcome when she wakes up in the morning. Or how she'd feel explaining the decision to someone older and wiser (like an aunt, uncle or grandparent). If the idea of explaining it to an adult she looks up to makes her feel afraid or sad, she knows it's probably a good idea to rethink before she acts. This is also a good way to sort of plant a bug in your teen's mind: when they have a big decision to make, they'll get a flash of someone older and wiser in their mind's eye, and often just wondering, "*What would my Aunt want me to do?*" can help guide them to smart choices.

Despite Outward Appearances, Teens Are **Listening**

✳ **Exclusive National Survey Results** ✳
Teens: Tell the Truth!

If my parents would just _____, I'd talk to them more honestly about my sex life.

Teens 12 to 17 respond:

I do talk honestly about my sex life with my parents	38%
Not overreact	23%
Don't know	15%
Not preach	13%
Listen to me more	7%
I would never talk honestly about my sex life with my parents	4%

"We know it's embarrassing for you as a parent—it's embarrassing for us as your teens! Just make it comfortable."

—Faith, 17, New Jersey

Most people I talk to who are gearing up for "the big talk" with a teen want to know how they should open up the conversation, what exactly to say, and how to say it. They usually time The Conversation based on what they perceive as the teen's readiness; maybe he or she is more interested in girls or guys these days, or maybe the teen is 14 and it just seems like the right time. One thing any honest teen will tell you is that by the time the adults around him start thinking about talking about sex with him, he's been ready to start having these kinds of conversations for *at least* six months—at least.

Many adults don't want to bring up the idea of sex with teens because they think that mentioning it to teens or preteens is giving the message, "I kind of expect you to be fooling around (or at least thinking about it)." This is an understandable concern, but it turns out to be unfounded. Interestingly, lots of teens tell me they don't want to bring up sex because they fear mentioning it will make their parents (or other adults they trust and confide in) assume they're doing it.

Talking about sex does not make teens want to do it, especially if the teen is connected to the parent and the parent is clear about his or her expectations. As Jeanne Stanley, director of the Bryson Institute of the Attic Youth Center in Philadelphia, puts it: "Talking does not necessarily mean action. If that were the case, then every time you said 'Pick up the clothes in your room,' that would happen. It doesn't." And as far as teens bringing it up, that doesn't necessarily mean they're doing it, either.

But before you begin to have these conversations about sex, some background information will help you mentally prepare (and if you're not convinced yet that you should have this conversation ASAP, the info you're about to read should convince you).

YOU MAY THINK YOU'VE ALREADY TALKED TO YOUR TEEN ABOUT SEX—BUT YOUR TEEN DOESN'T AGREE

University of Pennsylvania sociology professor Frank Furstenberg does an experiment with his freshman students every year. He asks them to take out a piece of paper and pen and write about the last conversation they had with their parents about sex.

His findings? "Many of the students at Penn either have never had a conversation or they've had a highly elliptical discussion full of warning and dangers," says Furstenberg. "It perpetuates this cycle—

the students all complained that they were not informed by their parents, and *their* parents too would complain that they weren't informed by *their* parents. We need to begin to break this cycle."

Even worse than the fact that teens feel they aren't getting enough information from their parents is the fact that parents incorrectly assume that they *are* giving enough information to their teens. To wit: although 90 percent of parents report having had a conversation about sex with their teen, nearly 4 in 10 teens say they have *never* discussed sex, contraception, or pregnancy with their parents.

✳ Evidence of the Parent-Teen ✳ Communication Gap

25% of teen girls and 46% of teen boys who have had sex
say their parents are in the dark about it.
28% have discussed sex with their parents,
but only after having sex.
20% have had their parents find out they were having sex,
but not from them.

Top Reasons for Not Talking to a Parent About Sex
(in order of popularity):
They worry about their parents' reaction.
They're worried their parents will think they're having sex.
They're embarrassed.
They don't know how to bring it up.
They don't think their parents will understand.
—Kaiser Family Foundation, 2002

WHAT YOU DON'T TELL TEENS ABOUT SEX THEY WILL TRY TO FIND OUT ELSEWHERE AND/OR MAKE UP

It's important when you're talking with teens to be as clear as possible, even though that makes these conversations all the more uncomfortable. You may think you've already put your feelings on the table by saying something like, "Well, if you ever have any questions . . . about anything . . . you can always ask me." But studies show that teens do not understand adults' more subtle ways of communication.

"Kids fill in the blanks wrong," says Robert Blum, M.D., Ph.D., chairman of the Department of Population and Family Health Sciences at the Johns Hopkins Bloomberg School of Public Health and co-investigator on the National Longitudinal Study of Adolescent Health, which is the largest survey of American youth. His most dramatic finding? "About a third of teens totally misread parental cues and messages. And they misread them in both directions. Kids are as likely to view their parents as more *approving* of sexual relationships than their parents might actually be or more *disapproving* than they might actually be. Kids are just, plain and simply, often misreading their parents." This dangerously poor communication can mean that a teen thinks you're not too concerned about who he dates or that you truly hate her boyfriend—or that you disapprove of her even kissing someone—when none of these in fact reflects your real feelings. Quite simply, it means that many parents think they've made their points perfectly clear, but that's not the case as far as their teen is concerned.

And miscommunication leads to misunderstandings and sneaky behavior. If he thinks you hate his girlfriend, he won't talk about her and may even be more driven to her because of "forbidden fruit" syndrome. If she thinks you'd kick her out of the house if she asked you about birth control . . . and so on. This is probably the most common misconception about parental reactions, by the way—"My mom (or dad) would *kill* me if they knew the truth about . . ." Here's a classic example:

"She'd disown me"

"I talk to my mom about who I like and how my friends are treating me, and my feelings on things and what I'm going through. I've asked her, 'Did you have sex before you got married?' and I guess she did because she got really mad and didn't want to answer. Mainly the things I don't tell her is when it comes to guys, like mistakes I've made. I'm ashamed. I know she said she'd be understanding, but I know she wouldn't be and then I would have the most strict rules ever and wouldn't be able to enjoy my high school life. She'd disown me or something."   —Mallory, 15, Missouri

So often teens predict a massive overreaction from their parents, which leads them to withhold information. This may explain why only about a third of parents of sexually experienced 14-year-olds are aware that their child has had sex. Many teens tell me that they later found out or realized that not only would their parents not have "killed them," they would have been quite understanding and helpful if they had known what was really going on. Teens whose parents talk openly with them about sex speak of this with pride and clearly have the impression that these discussions meant decisions regarding sex were important enough to parents to make it a topic of conversation.

"I do talk to my parents . . . my parents are cool"

"I do talk to my parents about relationships. I find it easy to talk to my parents because they have always been around for me to talk to. Usually at dinner we talk about the day, like what went on at school and about friends and relationships.

"My advice would be to say, 'I need to talk to you' or 'I have something I want to tell you, can you help me out, or listen to me?' I feel comfortable because it is just part of my life, the way I have been brought up. Yes, I'm a virgin. I don't think you should have sex until you are married. Right now I don't feel it is necessary to have sex, and my opinion right now is you should wait until you are married. My parents are cool—they are strict . . . but not too strict."

—Clay, 14, Minnesota

✳ When it comes to your decisions about sex, ✳ who is most influential?

Parents 45%

Friends 31%

Teachers/sex educators 5%

Religious leaders 3%

The media 4%

Siblings 5%

Someone else 1%

—The National Campaign to Prevent Teen Pregnancy, 2004

Keep in mind, though, as you have these discussions, that often teens can tolerate only a small amount of information at once. A few-sentence exchange can have more impact on them than trying to get them to have a sit-down chat on this topic for long stretches of time.

Parents Speak Out:
"My son was like 'Okay Mom! Enough!'"

"When my son was pretty young, he asked me one little question, and this was on a Sunday morning, precoffee, about how babies get born. I started telling him all about how they get conceived. I started to really get into it and was telling him all this stuff, apparently way more than he wanted to know, because he started to walk away! He was like 'Okay Mom! Okay! That's enough!' And I was so disappointed, I was like, 'Wait! I didn't even get to menstruation yet!'"

—Ohio mother of three teen boys

IF A TEEN DOESN'T THINK SHE CAN TALK OPENLY ABOUT SEX AND SEXUALITY, SHE'S FAR MORE LIKELY TO "SNEAK SEX."

Teens who feel like they can't talk openly with their parents about sex, contraception, and the emotions that go along with sexual acts are not any less likely to experiment. They are no less susceptible to their hormones or the onslaught of messages they get from friends, TV, movies, and the Internet. They're getting hundreds of messages a day about sex and sexuality, and if sex is not talked about openly at home, those are the *only* messages they're getting. And those messages can be confusing, even to the most clear-minded teenager.

"Uneducated teens make the wrong decisions"

"I'm 17 years old and extremely thankful that I'm finally a senior! I'm part of a peer-sex-ed council—a group of seniors trained in all the different aspects of sexuality, from STD's, contraception methods, to just discussing sex comfortably with other teens, parents, and members of the community.

"If a couple has been dating for over a month, there's a very good chance they are having sex. But so many teens are not educated in the topic of sex and make wrong decisions because they either know too little or have the wrong information. If you as a parent cannot talk to your child about sex, then make sure someone does. Do not leave it to sex ed. because the majority of schools do not provide the answers to the questions us teens have. We know it's embarrassing for you as a parent; it's embarrassing for us as your teens. I Just make it comfortable. It's the teens who know they can go to their parents with a sex question that practice responsible sex." —Faith, 17, New Jersey

Sociology professor Frank Furstenberg sums it up well when he says that as a society, Americans "both shake a very negative finger when it comes to talking about sexuality . . . and at the same time we infuse advertising, television and motion pictures with images of sex." Teens are left with a contradiction that makes sex seem simultaneously very exciting, very dangerous . . . and very taboo to discuss. The end result, unfortunately, is that we have teens experimenting with less of a base of solid information and the distinct feeling that talking about sex in a straightforward, information-seeking way is not permitted. Better to figure it out on your own, many teens report, and to only bring parents into the picture when a crisis emerges . . . if then.

WHEN TEENS SNEAK SEX, BAD THINGS HAPPEN

Let's face it, no one wants to imagine their child having sex. So it's easier to adopt a "this will sort itself out" mentality whereby you're ready to consider your child as a sexually active being . . . when they're 35 and married. While parents get used to the idea that teens may be thinking about sex, teens are forging ahead with exploring their sexuality—secretly. This sentiment, that parents don't know what their teens are really doing, sexually speaking, is supported by hard evidence. "Parents are pretty out of touch with a lot of their kids' sexual behaviors," says Dr. Blum. "Specifically, when we asked parents if their kids were having sex, we found that if they said yes, they were correct 97 percent of the time. On the other hand, if the parents said, 'No, my kid's not having sex,' the parents were correct just less than half of the time."

When you don't talk about sex in a clear and forthright way with teens, they get the message that sex is something to be hidden. They get the feeling that they're expected to handle issues surrounding sex on their own, and what they *don't* know they should figure out by asking their friends or their boyfriend/girlfriend or by surfing around on the Internet. Even though it feels wrong and sometimes scary to them, they get the distinct impression that their best move is to wing it.

"I feel weird hiding stuff from my mom"

"One thing I wish I could tell my parents is that things have changed so much in my mind. Sixth grade is no longer about boys having cooties like my parents remember. And if a bully is messing with you, you can't say something like 'I don't think your attitude is appropriate, and it is hurting my feelings' without getting beat up (at least in my school).

"I'm 14, and all my friends talk about dating but I'm not really allowed to until I'm like 16 or 17, but I've met so many guys with potential, and a few have even asked me out, but I keep turning them down mostly because I feel weird hiding a lot of my life from my family, especially my mom. We're pretty close.

"I keep thinking about finding the perfect guy and going further in the relationship once I think we're ready but I don't know because I'm kind of dumbfounded when it comes to stuff like that, and I'm afraid that if and when it happens, I'll mess something up.

I'm just not sure about much of anything anymore. I think these points are important because no one seems to listen to me when I try to tell someone. I've talked to my principal, my friends, and even my parents but to no avail. Please help me and many people who are wondering what to do when you want to knock some sense into your parents when it comes to some of these topics."

—Nadia, 14, Massachusetts

Sneaking sex often means teens are forging ahead, with no guidance and no solid information about how to avoid pregnancy, disease, even heartbreak. Teen after teen I talk with reports that even though they are open with their parents about other things, sex remains an area that isn't often discussed at home.

But just as being clear with your teen about your expectations can help ensure that your teen will make responsible decisions, being quiet about sex makes it more likely that you'll have no idea what's really going on in your teen's sex life. And this silence also greatly increases the enormous risk that your teen will make random, teenlogical decisions with potentially life-changing consequences, such as pregnancy, STDs, or unwanted sex.

When you consider that the average age for first sex in the United States is 16, and almost all young adults have had sex by age 20, it forces you to realize that you don't get to, ultimately, choose when your teen will have sex. Or with whom. Or how. Or even how they'll define "having sex."

You *can*, however, be a force for good in guiding your teenager to make smart choices. You can help to ensure that your teen respects himself/herself and their partner. You can help them make smart choices so they don't end up regretting their decisions or putting themselves at undue risk for unwanted sex, STDs, or pregnancy. In short, you can't make these choices for them, but you *can* be in their corner to help be sure they make the best possible choices for themselves.

TIP: What do you think your teen will be thinking about, regarding dating and sex, in two years? She is probably thinking about those things today, so start talking about them now.

REAL-WORLD ADVICE

So by now, hopefully you're convinced that having this conversation with your teen (or the teens in your life) is not only worthwhile, it's essential. But how to get started? Good news for the squeamish: you can start slowly. This is not about having One Big Conversation. It's about setting up communication between yourself and your teen so she feels comfortable talking with you about sex. And remember that science is on your side: study after study shows that you have the most influence over your teen's decisions about sex—more than their friends, their favorite shows, or their musical influences.

✳ The Power of Parents ✳

Teenagers who feel highly connected to their parents are far more likely to delay sexual activity than their peers.
Teenagers in grades 8 through 11 who perceive that their mother disapproves of their engaging in sexual intercourse are more likely than their peers to delay sexual activity.
—National Longitudinal Study of Adolescent Health, 2000

✳

87% of teens believe it would be easier for teens to postpone sexual activity and avoid teen pregnancy if they were able to have more open, honest conversations about these topics with their parents.
—The National Campaign to Prevent Teen Pregnancy, 2004

Talk the Talk: Teenagers Will Listen if You Say...

"I remember in high school there was one guy [or girl] who I adored, [name here]. I used to memorize his class schedule! He didn't know I was alive though, and that completely hurt. Do you know what I mean? Ever feel ignored by someone who is really important to you? Or have you ever felt like you're the only person in the world who felt a certain way?"

"I had a friend who told me that he wasn't a virgin, and I completely believed him because he had all the details about what it was like to lose your virginity. But you know what I found out years later? He was actually the last one of all of us to lose his virginity. You can't always believe what friends say about this stuff. Have you ever believed something and then found out it was a total lie? Did you ever feel like you wanted to lie about something to your friends? Why do you think people sometimes lie about who they're dating, or whether they've had sex?"

Before you start talking with your teen about sex, you may need to make some adjustments to the ways in which you and your teen communicate. If you two are constantly fighting this may take a little longer and/or you may want to consider enlisting a counselor to help the two of you talk in a more consistently civilized way. But if you feel like you have a fairly open relationship with your teen, these steps should help you make the minor adjustments necessary to set the stage for good communication about sex.

I listened when my parents said:

"Do not let anyone push you into something that you're not ready for."   —Girl, 17, Florida

PUT ON YOUR TEEN HAT

For a moment, think back to when you were a teenager. Not the happy-glorified part when you got the perfect date to the prom or you were the lead singer in the band and the girls were dying for you and life was great. Think about any negative, insecurity-inducing moments you had as a teen. Bad skin, dates gone wrong, horrific dance moves, unrequited crushes . . . If you find yourself cringing, you are in the right frame of mind. Try to stay in that emotional place for a minute and look at yourself, today. Does your teen-self want to come to you for answers or confide in you? If no, why not? Do you look ready to judge or yell? These questions might help you adjust the face you show to your teen.

"Sometimes I think that my mom has forgotten how it felt the first time she met my dad," says Kaitlynn, 15. "The way he looked at her, the way he talked to her. I know I'm only 15, but I want to experience that. Not go sleeping around, but to have that one special guy."

Showing your teen that you remember what it's like to be her age will make her more receptive to what you have to say. Even if you're expressing how different things are now from when you were a teen, many of the feelings will still resonate.

TIP: Don't be put off by long silences or your teen saying he doesn't want to talk. Say: "I really want to know your answer to this," and then wait for him to answer, even if it takes five minutes. You will develop a new groove of communication if you are patient.

Remember how intense your feelings were as a teen—and how you felt like no one could possibly understand what you were feeling . . . and how lonely that could make you feel. "The only thing I could possibly ask is for my parents to understand," says Raina, 16, from Michigan. "They think it's just a little fling, that it's impossible to find love at my age. My dad even tries to tell me to break up with my boyfriend now because 'high school relationships never last.' Why can't they be optimistic, realize how much my boyfriend means to me, and hope for the best for us? All I want is for them to be supportive."

And remember, when you're preparing to talk to your teen, that this is not about trying to be cool. Teens do not want or expect the adults around them to be cool. This is about being approachable, reliable, focused, and in touch with your teenager. You might find it helpful to keep checking back with your "inner teen" while reading over the next few tips so you can imagine how you'll be seen by your teenager.

TIP: Accept that candid, effective communication about sex with your teen may result in your teen thinking you're "uncool." Small price to pay for a teen who acts responsibly.

PRACTICE NOT JUDGING

Judging is a big issue for teens. They hate to feel judged (and really, doesn't everyone?). Surprisingly, even people who are extraordinarily nonjudgmental in their day-to-day lives can have a hard time not judging their own child when he or she is relating their life experiences. Since you've already survived your teen years, it can be excruciatingly hard to listen to your teenager when you can tell after the first few words out of her mouth that what she wants to do (or who she wants to date, or where she wants to go) is a huge mistake.

But the second your face (or worse, your voice) registers "this is stupid," your teen will hit the "off" switch and stop sharing with you. Rosemary Prentice is a family nurse practitioner on the faculty at the University of Southern Maine. Every year she sees hundreds of teens who feel comfortable asking her questions they would never ask their parents. "They want to be able to ask their questions without worrying if somebody's going to judge them based on what they ask or the stuff they've done," Prentice says.

TIP: Ignore your teen's expressions, even if he rolls his eyes at you. He is listening, no matter what faces he's making.

But how can you stop judging—or at least appear as if you're not judging? In the beginning, this will be all about appearances. As much as it may pain you, try not giving advice the next time your teen comes to you to tell you about what's going on in his life. Just listen. Listen to him tell you all about the jerk in his math class who got him in trouble even though he wasn't doing anything, and about how he asked one girl to the dance and now a girl he likes better seems to have a crush on him, and about how he needs, *needs* a new car before January because that's when everyone else in his class will have turned 17 and he'll be the only living teenager without his own wheels. You may find (surprise!) that he doesn't want advice. He may just want you to hear what he's saying and he'll figure some of this stuff out on his own.

The hardest part of this is that your teen will make mistakes this way. Let him. These are the kinds of mistakes that will teach him how to be a stronger person. (Of course, the caveat here is if you think he plans to do something illegal, dangerous, or immoral, by all means step in.) Listening is key to opening the door for positive communication, says Elizabeth Casparian, who has her Ph.D. in educational leadership in human sexuality from the University of Pennsylvania and spent five years answering teens' questions about sexuality for the award-winning Rutgers University website Sex, Etc. "If you're really listening and showing that you're listening and not always having to put in your own two cents here and there, then the teen is going to keep talking," Casparian says.

> ## *Talk the Talk: Teenagers Will Listen if You Say...*
>
> "Listen, it's my job to be sure you don't get hurt, so that's why I'm listening so closely to what you're saying, but most of all, I'm really glad you're telling me all this. I want to hear more. What happened after she didn't call back? Did you feel like you were still interested in her, or did you feel like that was the last straw or what?"

While you're listening (and not talking) pay attention to your thoughts and the things you're *dying* to say out loud. How do you sound to yourself? Is it like, *You* know *you did something to provoke your teacher so don't feed me* that *and it's so* wrong *to ask one girl and then go with another, and you do* not *need a car. When I was your age . . . ?* How would your teen self feel being talked to this way? Judged? Aren't you glad you kept quiet?

I listened when my parents said:
"When you have sex you become one with that person, and being one with a person is not casual . . . it's very serious."

—Boy, 17, Vermont

And remember that to your teen, even the mildest "suggestion" can be viewed as judging, in-their-face, scolding. "I have parents who I can't talk to about anything because I get yelled at for everything I say. It is hopeless," says Jane, 13, from New York. "It's like my dad doesn't understand that I am a child, I will make mistakes, and I am not perfect. I wish that he would understand that." If you get the sense that your teen is shutting down or feeling scolded, bring it up so it's on the table. You might even have to walk away from the conversation for a few hours or a few days. Just leave the door open when you do. "Let your kids know that you're there for them if they ever need anything," suggests Ike, 16, from Nebraska. "Let them know you respect their choices . . . just remind them: for every action, there is a consequence."

DECIDE ON YOUR MESSAGE

One of the reasons it's so intimidating to talk to teens about sex is that it's hard to know exactly what message you're "supposed" to give. You don't have to worry about being too early on this conversation or giving too much information; your teen will let you know what he or she is ready to hear. So take a moment to talk with your husband, wife, colleague, or partner-in-parenting and really think, in concrete terms, about what you would like your teenager to do or not do. You're not going to share this plan with your teen (not yet), but it's important that you be as honest as you can with yourself and with each other at this juncture. It doesn't matter what your beliefs are about premarital sex or hooking up—these tips will help you talk to your teen about whatever your values are. But it is important for you to be clear at the outset what your expectations are for your teen.

Some examples of concrete expectations parents shared with me include: "Before he has sex, I feel it's important that he be in a committed relationship with someone who cares about him," and "I don't expect her to have sex until after high school." Remember that for expectations to have an impression, they have to be very clear. So "Wait until you're in love" won't work, but "Wait until you're X age, you've been dating your boyfriend/girlfriend for at least a year, are in love, and you're able to speak openly with your boyfriend/girlfriend about birth control, STD prevention, and how sex might change the relationship" will.

Once you've agreed upon your message and you feel comfortable with it, give your teen an assignment. Make up a list of questions (or use the ones that follow) that point to your teen's values, and hand them to him. Ask him to write down his answers and not show them to you, or anyone, unless he wants to. This way you're being clear with him about your thoughts and beliefs about sex, while helping him internalize his own thoughts and values. Most teenagers don't think very much about sex in a reality-based way until the moment it happens, which is problematic for a variety of reasons that are explored throughout this book. You are helping your teenager think about sex in advance and create a value system that will help responsibly guide his choices.

Sample questions:

- **What do I imagine sex will be like?**

- **How do I expect to feel after I have sex for the first time?**

- **What are my hopes, fears, concerns, and wishes about sex?**

- **Who do I hope to have sex with for the first time?**

- **How will I know that the time and person are right?**

- **What will give me clues that the time or person are not right?**

- **What kinds of issues should be discussed before a relationship becomes sexual?**

KNOW THAT THIS WILL BE THE FIRST OF A SERIES OF DISCUSSIONS

Even if you are just starting to talk to your teen or preteen about sex for the first time, you're going to get best results (meaning your child understands your values and has the tools she needs to make smart decisions) if you start a conversation and keep the door open for the conversation to continue over the coming days, weeks, months, and years. Look at this as an ongoing dialogue, not a monologue that you recite and then are happy it's over with and feel you "did it."

TIP: Try talking to your teen about sex when you're driving in a car together. That way you don't have to look each other in the eye—and he can't walk away from you if the conversation gets uncomfortable.

> ## Talk the Talk: Teenagers Will Listen if You Say...
>
> "I care about you so much that I want to be sure you're careful with your life, so I'm going to be bringing up the topic of sex and dating and asking you questions. Sometimes you'll feel like I'm in your face about it, but it's so important that I have to say these things even though it can be embarrassing. It's important that we talk about sex and dating because soon enough, you are going to be making decisions that can affect the rest of your life, and you'll be making them without me around—I want to be sure you're prepared to act smart."

"I think the talk that we're all familiar with is often sort of this one-shot deal," says Jennifer Oliphant, community outreach coordinator for the National Teen Pregnancy Prevention Research Center at the University of Minnesota. "The kid knows that 'if I just endure this, I won't have to listen to it again.'" But this is a recipe for the teen tuning out to what you have to say. "There is also research that shows that parents think they've talked about it, and the kids say they haven't," says Kristin Moore, Ph.D., president of the nonprofit research think tank Child Trends. "And so parents really can't rush right through it. It has to be a conversation that happens over a period of time."

Think about when your boss (or your own parent) says something to you that you don't want to hear—you kind of tune out until it's over and then move on with your day. But if your boss kept bringing up the same topic and asking for your input, you're forced to participate in the conversation and, to some degree, deal with the issue at hand.

GIVE TEENS PERMISSION TO TALK
This is the gratifying part because it's easy and it works right away. The next time you and your teenager are having a good time together,

say, "You know, you can always come to me if you need advice or help with anything, about your friends or life or school, or even sex." Then pause, and don't be discouraged by your teen's look of horror or disgust. Just continue: "And if you don't feel comfortable talking to me, you can always consult (name of adult you trust here)." Be sure to clear it with the adult before you offer the teen his or her name so no one gets caught off-guard.

TIP: Tell your teen you trust her to make smart decisions. Let her know you view her as responsible and careful with her life, and she will strive to live up to this reputation.

It's important when you're having this (and any) discussion with your teen that you also keep in mind your nonverbal signals. Try not to cross your arms or twist your legs together or give any other sign that this discussion is the last thing you want to be doing right now. And then, this is the icing on the cake: "I might not always have an answer for you right away, but I will always find out the answer for you or tell you where to get the answers you need. It's important to me that you know you can always ask me anything."

Parents Speak Out:
"I made my husband talk to my son about it"

"When my son was 15, I started all of a sudden finding my creams were missing—like my expensive face creams, the good stuff. And I was like: What's going on? I'd find mostly used tubes of my creams behind the TV or various other places around the house. I told my husband that he had to tell my son *he* found the cream—I didn't think my son would want to talk to his mom about masturbation. My husband took my son aside and just said, listen, this is something that has to stay in the bedroom, this is okay to do but it's a private activity, and if you need creams, you can go to the store and buy them or ask me to bring you appropriate creams—but stay away from Mom's expensive stuff."

—Rhode Island mother of an 11-year-old girl and 16-year-old boy

Initiating these conversations is going to be difficult, and it's going to feel awkward. That's normal. Your teenager is going to react to this awkwardness by making faces or acting like he doesn't want to talk to you. Instead of reacting to this reaction, acknowledge to yourself that this is uncharted territory, and it's going to feel a little weird, but if you can move through the awkwardness, you're going to bring your relationship with your teenager to a whole new level.

THE LAST WORD

By opening the door, you're giving your teen the message that information about sex and sexuality is not taboo in your household. You're saying that you will listen to her and respect her for having questions. You don't have to use these exact scripts, but remember that statistic about how teens so often misinterpret what adults say and try to be as clear as you can be so you're sure your teen completely understands. And once you've opened that door, pause. Your teen may bring up something then and there. (Don't forget that you gave yourself an out by saying you might not have all the answers. If you're not ready to talk now, just tell him you'll get back to him. Then do.) Or he may just put his headphones back into his ears, stare into his cereal, and mutter, "Okay, whatever."

Either way, he's heard you.

Parents Have a Say in When (and How) Teens Lose Their **Virginity**

✳ Exclusive National Survey Results ✳ Tell the Truth! Testimony

The one thing my parents said that had the most impact on my decision about virginity was:

"The amount of diseases that are out there."   —Boy, 14, Louisiana

✳

"That I'm just not ready."   —Girl, 13, Indiana

✳

"Be your own person."   —Boy, 12, New York

✳

"I should lose my virginity with the person that I think I would spend the rest of my life with."   —Girl, 17, Georgia

✳

"Being pregnant is forever."   —Girl, 13, Washington

✳

"You can talk to me about anything and I promise not to get mad."
   —Boy, 12, North Carolina

✳

"Always put your education first."   —Girl, 13, Kentucky

*

"If you get her pregnant, it will be hard to finish school."

—Boy, 17, South Carolina

*

"Your self-esteem and reputation are the most important things for you to keep intact."   —Girl, 17, Texas

*

"That I am the most important person and the decision should be mine."   —Boy, 17, New Mexico

*

"Mom told me about losing her own virginity too young."

—Girl, 16, Oklahoma

*

"Make it meaningful."   —Boy, 16, Maryland

*

"If I do it, I can't go back and change it. I have to respect myself."

—Girl, 15, Pennsylvania

*

"Follow your heart. . . . We trust you."   —Boy, 16, Pennsylvania

No matter how open a family's communication style, a teen will almost never approach a parent to ask: "How do I know if I'm ready for sex?" But after editing teen-sex-advice columns for years, I can tell you this is one of the most frequent questions teens have asked me. So we can safely assume that, on their own, most teenagers are not sure how to tell if they're ready for sex. A teen may, along with her friends, come up with her own rules about what signifies readiness, such as being in a serious relationship or feeling like she's in love. Or he may, like so many teens I know, feel like at a certain age you really should just "do it" and get your virginity over with. As Ruby, 17, puts it: "I could tell my parents that I'm okay with my virginity but I couldn't share the fact that I would like to lose it before I become a freakishly old virgin." Makes you wonder what a teen's idea of "freakishly old" is, doesn't it?

Keep in mind that parents do have a say here, because teens are looking to their parents for direction and a clear message on this topic. (To have maximum impact on your teen's decisions, though, it's best not to wait until you think your teen may be having sex or on the brink of having sex to start bringing it up.) But it's not enough just to talk about sex and what your hopes are for your teen. In our efforts to ensure teens makes smart decisions in this realm, there is a force working against us: teens develop theories, misconceptions, and attitudes about virginity loss that can be detrimental to our goal of getting them to delay sex until they're ready, and having those who are sexually active take steps to protect against pregnancy and STDs.

These sometimes take the form of myths that many teens hold to be true, such as:

TEEN VIRGINITY MYTH #1: "I'M GOING TO REGRET MY FIRST TIME NO MATTER WHAT"

Aside from the obvious risks of pregnancy and STDs, there are emotional risks involved with having sex. You have probably heard the statistic that 66 percent of teens regret their first sexual experience, and many of the teens who have contacted me do regret their first time. Why so much regret? This is an area that's hard to study in a scientific way, so I can only tell you what I hear from the hundreds of teens I'm in touch with. Of course anyone who gets forced into having sex regrets it. Girls and guys who get pressured into having sex regret it (yes, guys get pressured too, especially by their friends). Girls and guys who thought they were in love but become dissatisfied with the way the relationship evolves (or devolves) after sex regret it. If a girl has sex and her reputation gets tarnished she regrets it; this is less of a risk for boys, whose reps tend to get enhanced by sex.

TIP: An easy and important thing to say to your teen is that if she's unsure if she's ready for sex, she will never regret waiting.

Those are the ways teens make each other regret having sex. But the whole adult threat of "You're going to regret it" is a double-edged sword. It's important to be careful about the messages we give to teens about what it means to be sexually active. We don't want to give teens the message that sex is a terrifying and impossible-to-navigate landscape of bad feelings and disease. The end result of this kind of talk is a teen who figures, *Well, since it's going to be a bad experience anyway, I might as well just get it over with.*

"Your first time is never magical"

"I'm from Long Island, and I'm 16 years old. I'm a 34D and have beautiful brown hair. I'm a good height and I'm not really ugly. If I really wanted to I could find a boyfriend, but the thing is, I don't. A lot of girls like to wait for their first time to be with someone they love because they want it to be 'magical.' But your first time is never magical. It hurts like hell, and it's nothing like what it's talked up to be. So I figure that if you do it safely with condoms and all that a few times before you find your true love or first love, when you do find your first love or true love it will feel good and then it will be magical."
                                                      —Anne, 16, New York

Besides, it's simply not true that sex is always a bad thing; almost everyone would agree that at some point, under the right circumstances, sex is a good thing, a positive thing. And when she figures this out, which may be sooner than you'd hoped, you'll have lost all credibility if you've made sex out to be a horrible thing. Also keep in mind that your teen may in fact not be a virgin. If you're constantly saying that girls who do it always get branded sluts, what message are you sending to her?

This is not to say in any way that the message parents should give to teens should be pro-teen sex. Rather, you need to be careful what you say to your teen, who may be sexually active and not telling you, so you don't give him the impression that if he's sexually active, your opinion of him will drastically change and his life is basically over. You also paint yourself into a corner if you threaten a teen with regret and then she has sex and feels great about it—again, you'll have lost all credibility. Finally, if a teen feels like the first time is going to be regrettable or, as they might put it, "suck" no matter what, it feeds their theory that it's best to "just get it over with." A better idea is to discuss the idea of regret and how to avoid it, and what specific kinds of actions or situations generally do (and don't) lead to regret (there are specific examples later in this chapter in the "Real-World Advice" section).

I listened when my parents said:

"I have to be responsible for my actions."   —Boy, 17, Texas

TEEN VIRGINITY MYTH #2: "LOSING YOUR VIRGINITY IS SOMETHING THAT 'JUST HAPPENS'"

As mentioned in Chapter 1, too often sex is something that "just happens" among teens without much planning or forethought. Why is sex "just happening" to our teenagers? In our culture you don't have to look very critically at movies or TV shows to see that the whole idea of being "swept away" is highly valued—it's the preferred way for someone to have sex, when they're just so moved by love and swooning that the sex is simply inevitable. Added to that strong cultural pressure is the inhibition-lowering powers of alcohol and/or simply the intoxicating feeling of doing something incredibly exciting, new, and potentially against your parents' wishes, and it's a recipe for sex that "just happens."

"His smooth words melted me like ice cream"

"I'm 15 but still deal with the same problems with my love life as adults. You think he's the one, and realistically he's not. When he's with you he acts one way and when he's with his friends he acts another. You want to give yourself to him because you don't want him to stray, but in your mind you're always thinking, *Hey, what if this is one of his tricks just to get in your pants?* But his lies are so well told, as if they were the truth.

"So you tell an aunt, and she's like, 'Well, sweetie, I think you should wait until you're married. What do you know about love? Just wait.'

"So now you put up a wall with him and his lies, you know thinking, *He ain't gettin' none.* But when you see him your wall is bombed. The smoothness of his words are melting you like ice cream on a hot day. So he starts kissing on your neck and telling you how good you look and you're loving every minute of it. So your panties start getting wet and he starts fondling with you and rubbing between your legs and you never felt anything like this before. So he lays you on his bed and he's telling you, 'Girl, I love you.' So your head hits the pillow, and you're still shaking, then you feel a hard thrust in you. It's not like how you imagined. It's worse. You feel like crying, and he's getting excited, finally he ejects, and you're so happy its over.

"And he's now bragging about how good it felt, and he's talking about doing it again. Now you regret that you ever met him because you see him for the dickhead he really is. A mistake that could have been avoided if your hormones weren't pumping."

—Sydney, 15, New York

If, like Sydney, a teen is going to have sex, it's vital that they protect themselves. If they are hoping, however, for that "swept away" feeling, it's far less likely that they'll be toting condoms or have started taking the Pill one month in advance. Being "swept away,"

Child Trends' president Kristin Moore, Ph.D., stresses, "from a public health point of view, is not a good thing."

Being "swept away" or "caught up in the moment" also carries with it very real health risks. If you're not expecting to have sex, why be prepared with a condom? This could explain the finding (by researchers from Columbia and Yale that teens who take a virginity pledge do delay sex, but are one third more likely to have unprotected sex if they break the pledge (the same researchers reported in 2004 that 88 percent of pledges end up having premarital sex). The next-day realization that they've exposed themselves to STDs and possible pregnancy can bring feelings of regret and fear. And there are emotional risks to the "swept away" syndrome as well—teenagers may be more likely to regret a decision they made on the spur of the moment, based on desire and hormones, that may go against their beliefs or run contrary to what they had hoped losing their virginity would be like.

TIP: Your teen *will* ask you how and when you lost your virginity. Be ready with your answer. (It's okay to say "I don't feel comfortable sharing that with you.")

In contrast to many girls' desire to have a romantic, swooning first sexual experience, many boys tell me that it's simply considered cooler to have sex than to be a virgin, and they view their virginity as something to "get over with."

"The sooner you lose it, the better"

"I'm a virgin, but if you're a virgin at my school, it's a big deal because guys think virginity is a joke. The sooner you lose it the better. The people who have had sex are considered cooler than the others. A lot of guys don't have girlfriends; they just have one-night stands. People who haven't had sex are either doing it for moral reasons or because they haven't found the right one yet."   —Roman, 17, Ohio

"Virginity is pretty much only important to girls"

"I go to a school where everyone knows everything about each other. If something happens between two people, by the end of the day everyone will know about it. People date and some have serious relationships; some don't. I only talk about my relationships with my mom when she asks and asks. The conversations are short and awkward.

"Virginity is pretty much only important to girls. I think that's how it is at most schools. What I mean is that guys just want to do it—we don't care if we're in love or anything. Only girls want to wait for the right person. With my group of friends, people have sex at parties. Sometimes it's couples, but usually it's just random hookups."   —Jason, 15, Connecticut

And of course, there is also some pressure among girls to "get with the program already" and start having sex, especially as they reach senior year in high school. Many girls say that it's harder to stay virgins, and that there is a lot of subtle pressure from friends and partners to have sex.

"No one wants to be the last one"

"No one wants to be the last one amongst their peers or friends to lose their virginity or still have it. People sometimes treat you as if having your virginity is a curse. Most people—well, the people who live in my community—expect to lose their virginity as soon as they think they're in a serious relationship or someone says 'I love you.' Most people lose it around 14 or 15, but I swear every year it gets younger.

"They don't attach any special meaning to it; they want to fit in with everyone or seem more mature, and everyone I know is eager to not be one. I am a virgin and quite proud and sad at the same time for being one. When I tell people I'm a virgin, they assume I'm not telling the truth. Some say I don't look like I am one (a virgin has a look?), some ask me if and when I want to lose it, and others, mostly boys, want to be the ones to take it away, which is a little disturbing. I don't sit and plan when I would like to lose it and with whom, but I feel this pressure increasing as I get older because to me it seems so rare to be my age and a virgin. I'm happy to tell people 'yeah, I am' because it proves that I'm a strong person, but then I feel alienated and sometimes wish I wasn't the person I am.

"I see my virginity as something very special and attached to me. I will not give it up to a one-night stand. I won't put myself in uncompromising situations, but I do want to lose it, eventually, as long as I'm 100 percent comfortable and ready.

"Should I feel so left out and alone just because I'm a virgin? I can't help but feel worse the older I get."   —Ruby, 17, New York

This teen's feeling, that "every year it gets younger and younger," is widely echoed by teens across the country. Many say they look back at the grades below them and feel like those kids are moving much faster than they were. As for those girls who are having sex at a young age, many are doing so with partners who are much older.

✳ How "the older partner" factors in: ✳

13% of relationships between same-age partners includes intercourse.

26% of relationships with a partner who is 2 years
older includes intercourse.

33% of relationships with a partner who is 3 years
older includes intercourse.

47% of relationships with a partner who is 4 or more years older
includes intercourse.

—NCTPTP/Child Trends, 2003

Girls often want to date older guys (and some boys also "date up," but it's far more rare). But there is an important distinction that parents need to make between a teen who has a slightly older partner (1 to 2 years, depending on the age and emotional maturity of the teen) and a teen who's getting together with someone older who may really be only interested in "One Thing." Because, as the above statistics suggest, the age spread between partners is a significant factor in indicating whether the relationship may become sexual. Older partners often have access to a car (meaning more privacy), money, and resources that can be very appealing to a younger teen. But by the very nature of their age difference, older partners are usually ready for more of an emotional and sexual committment than their younger partner, which can lead to an unequal relationship where one feels frustrated and the other feels pressured.

TEEN VIRGINITY MYTH #3: "VIRGINITY IS A GIFT TO BE GIVEN TO MY PARTNER FOR HIS/HER BIRTHDAY (OR GRADUATION, OR PROM . . .)"

Teens, like adults, plan big surprises for each other around major events, such as prom, graduation, New Year's Eve, and special birthdays and anniversaries. "We know that June is a big peak month for first sex," says Kristin Moore, Ph.D., "and it's always been my hypothesis that it's around prom." And the director of a health clinic told me that each year, starting in March, her staff likes to say, "Better gear up, the prommers are coming!" Prom night is a time when many new and exciting things happen. It may be a teen's first time wearing formal wear, going out all night on a date. It feels like "special exception" night, and one of those special exceptions is having sex for the first time.

✳ Exclusive National Poll Results ✳ Teens: Tell the Truth!

Do any of your friends plan to have sex for the first time on prom night?
1 in 5 17-year-olds say YES.

A study published in the *Journal of Marriage and Family* showed that teens who are part of a couple often have sex for the first time in December. New Year's Eve? Christmas? We can only guess. Even dates and anniversaries that seem arbitrary to us can resonate with teens. One girl told me that she was having a hard time talking with her mother about her boyfriend but she was going to confide in her mother fully, "once he and I have been together for six months. It'll just feel like everything's more real then."

It's wise to be aware of the days and dates that are important to your teenager and his friends/school/girlfriend. It's also a good idea to be clear with teenagers that it's not okay for someone to expect or demand virginity as a gift for a special occasion.

"Valentine's Day"

"I was never a part of the Girls Who Lose Virginity at an Early Age bandwagon. In fact, I grew up despising them, complaining that they were tainting the reputation of teendom. Sex never crossed my mind. I found it despicable and thought I had a right to look down on them for it.

"Then, I met my boyfriend. Now, I've heard stories of girls saying, 'Oh, we fell in love really quickly and it's true love!' and I never gave them much credit. Having experienced it, they now get the benefit of the doubt. My boyfriend and I fell in love almost instantly, and things moved quickly. I had never felt really comfortable in relationships, but with him I could do or say anything and not worry about what it would look like or how I would sound. We were truly in love. I knew that I wanted to be with him, and he told me the same thing every day.

"That's the crux of how, on that upcoming Valentine's Day, I ceased to be a virgin. There was no pressure or anxiety. It was a mutual decision that we knew we were both ready to make, and we understood the importance of it. I felt so comfortable with him, and it was more than just about the hormones. It was such a special thing to lose my virginity to the person I loved, and having him lose his right back to me, and it wasn't the dirty or repulsive deed I had imagined; it was beautiful and driven by love.

"I'm still with my boyfriend, and we plan to be together for the rest of our lives. I have no regrets about losing my virginity as a teenager, and I no longer look down on people just because they have. I understand the beautiful side of sex, the side that rarely gets the spotlight, the side that's overshadowed by mistakes. Although I have no regrets and have no guilt about being sexually active, I still realize the importance of the decision, and it's definitely not one to be taken lightly, and the decision is special and different for every person. I'm just grateful to have shared it with the person I love."   —Clara, 16, Florida

---

TIP: Communicate your hopes for your teen's behavior (including how long he stays a virgin) as wishes, not demands. If you make sex too much of a "forbidden fruit," you can unwittingly drive your teen toward it.

REAL-WORLD ADVICE

Talking to your teen about virginity means talking a lot about planning. Teens have a different idea of planning than adults do, which is to say it's very hard for them to plan too far into the future. (Ever try to ask a 10th grader where he wants to go for college?) It's also difficult for teens, developmentally, to project themselves into the future and anticipate consequences.

"But the failure to project oneself into the future has huge consequences," says Robert Blum, M.D., Ph.D., chairman of the Department of Population and Family Health Sciences at the Johns Hopkins

Bloomberg School of Public Health, who has written more than 220 journal articles, book chapters, and special reports on the study of adolescent health. "It is why the group who is most likely to become pregnant is the group who has already been pregnant. It's why kids who become pregnant never 'learn from their mistakes,' that's assuming that it was a *mistake* to begin with but what it really is, is a failure of *planning*."

So your first goal in talking with a teen about virginity is to get them to internalize a better planning process so that when it comes time to make decisions (should I or shouldn't I have sex/use birth control/take steps to prevent STDs), they'll be making smart choices. Planning is a good thing to talk about even if your teen is not sexually active, for obvious reasons, but if your teen is already having sex or might start having sex soon, please read the planning advice in this chapter. It's also important that you read Chapter 9 and get the "Real-World Advice" for how to talk to your teen about pregnancy and STD prevention as soon as possible.

GIVE A REALITY CHECK

Teens hate the idea of peer pressure. Simply using that phrase is a good way to get a teen to put on his headphones and look out the window. Still, it exists—often not in a blatant way, but subtly. Even though you always want to encourage your teen to be his own person and make his own decisions, you can use peer pressure to your advantage. Polling data from The National Campaign to Prevent Teen Pregnancy shows most teens agree that if they knew fewer teens were sexually active, it would be easier for them to delay sex. So here's your evidence: 68 percent of teens in grades 9 to 12 believe most teens their age have had sex, but less than half of teens are, in fact, sexually active. If you casually drop this tidbit into your conversation, say, on the drive to school one day, you're injecting a little reality-based information that will seep into his subconscious.

Talk the Talk: Teenagers Will Listen if You Say...

"You know, there are some things in life that require a lot of forethought and planning because they are the kind of events you don't want any surprises with. Can you think of any examples of what I'm talking about? Right: Like a big game. Or a dance. Or sex. Sex is the kind of thing you don't want to 'just happen' because you're swept up in the moment, because that can lead to regret or consequences like unintended pregnancy or STDs. That's why, even if you're abstinent right now (which is what we want for you), when you are ready for sex (which I hope won't be until [whatever your goal for your teen is here]), I hope you'll plan for it and think about possible consequences and how to prevent them before you're in the moment. What kinds of things should you think about before you get in a situation where you have to make a decision about sex?" Let your teen come up with some answers here, but help by making some suggestions if he doesn't know where to start: birth control, STD prevention, his morals and values, how he'll feel the next day, what kind of relationship he's in, why the decision is being made now . . . are all factors to consider.

"I was thinking that, especially these days, I bet it can be hard to tell how to know if you're really ready for sex. I hope you won't have sex until [your goal here]. But there's a list of things I'd like you to consider first that will help you figure out when you are ready. Take a look: [you can type up your own questions or use the ones in "Are You Ready for Sex" that follow]. I'd like you to answer these questions. You don't have to show me your answers, but I hope they will help you sort out your feelings and make smart decisions. If you want to talk about this more, I will be glad to." If you're more comfortable, you can write this as a note and leave it with the "Are you ready for sex" list under your teen's door or on his pillow.

TALK ABOUT THE IMPORTANCE OF PLANNING

How is your teenager at planning for homework? Is she always rushing around at the last second, doing schoolwork on the bus? Or does
she read 10 pages a night so the book's done two days before the report is due? If she's a real planner, it doesn't necessarily mean she'll
plan wisely for sex, because there are not a lot of hormonal or
partner-pressure factors when it comes to homework. However, it
does mean that you can use her planning style as a jumping-off point
for talking about planning, as in, "Remember how you . . . and that
worked out . . . ?"

Of course, if he's the worst planner in the world, this could sound
preachy, so in that case, begin by talking about planning as a general
topic, as something that everyone needs to practice because it's a very
important life skill.

✳ Why teens say no to sex: ✳

**30% say worries about pregnancy and STDs
have the greatest influence on their decisions about sex.
34% say morals, values, and religious beliefs
have the greatest influence.
—National Campaign to Prevent Teen Pregnancy, 2003**

Are you ready for sex?

• **Are you ready to talk honestly and openly with your partner about
birth control and STD prevention?** Both you and your partner need to
be comfortable with this discussion, because it takes two to implement birth control and STD-prevention plans.

• **Being sexually active means going to the doctor, getting an exam
and regular testing for STDs, even if you're using protection—are you
ready to do this?** The doctor I think we should see is Dr.
_____. And her phone number is _____. Before you

become sexually active you'll need to call and set up an appointment to see her. I can go with you if you'd like, or I can drop you off.

• **Do you have a plan to avoid STDs? Do you have a plan to prevent pregnancy?** What is the plan? Remember that it's up to you, not your partner, because I trust you—you need to be the one to buy the birth control and know how to use it. How will you carry out your plan, and how will you be sure you can carry it out every single time you have sex?

• **Are you interested in sex because you're ready or because you think other people want you to?** In other words, if your boyfriend/girlfriend or friends were not having sex, would you still want to have sex?

• **Are you mostly interested in sex when alcohol is around?** Of course, I hope you won't drink, but please know that alcohol can cloud your judgment and make you less inhibited. Remember, the next day you'll be sober again, so always think about how you'll feel then.

MODEL PLANNING

Teens learn planning from watching other people plan. So try to involve your teenager in any planning, especially the kind of planning where you have to think about consequences. He needs practice seeing that people plan for important decisions, in part by anticipating possible outcomes and planning for them. Many parents don't involve their teenager in family decisions because ultimately their opinion won't be enough to sway, say, whether the family moves to Pennsylvania for Mom's new job. But you're missing out on a great opportunity by leaving out your teen. Let him see that you're struggling with the option of leaving his school or finding a new position for Dad.

"There are a few reasons why kids can plan," says Dr. Blum.

Talk the Talk: Teenagers Will Listen if You Say...

"If we're going to get down to the beach this weekend, everyone's going to have to pack their own bag. Make a list of everything that's crucial (like sunglasses, bathing suit, etc.). Then think about what you'll want to wear each day and night and which things you could wear more than once so you don't overpack. I'm going to bring x, y, and z. Please put all your stuff on your bed, and I'll check it out before you pack it up just to be sure you don't forget anything important."

"One is they come from families that plan. I'm talking about planning for anything. I'm talking about putting money in a bank and planning for what we call a rainy day. Is there a culture in the house for planning, and do they talk about planning? That's how kids learn about planning, because they experience it in their environment."

Anytime you show your teen that you are planning ahead, projecting yourself into the future and weighing consequences, from something as simple as making a list for the store to something as major as planning a speech, he is learning how to do the same.

ENCOURAGING ABSTINENCE

Assuming that the message you developed after reading Chapter 1 includes some degree of "Don't have sex," whether it's "not until you're in love" or "not until you're out of high school" or "not until you're married," there is far more to planning abstinence than "Just say no." If it is important to you that your teenager choose abstinence, it's not just a matter of telling him to say no, because that doesn't prepare him for the challenges he'll face. You need to help him project his thinking into the future, to think about what it'll be like to be with a girl and want to have sex but choose not to. You need to arm him with things to think about, say, and do so he's really prepared to be abstinent. In other words, to help your teen choose abstinence, you need to talk about sex . . . a lot.

"I think sex 'just happens' a lot of the time," says Elizabeth Casparian, Ph.D., director of educational programs at the New Jersey–based teen health center HiTOPS. "Because teens really think, 'Okay, this is what I'm going to do: I'm gonna say no,' but in the heat of the moment, it takes a lot." Casparian offers some good tips to give teens who are planning for abstinence, such as coming up with rules for themselves in advance of "the moment."

What kind of rules? Maybe it's not being alone with a boyfriend or girlfriend in the backseat of the car, or not being alone in the house. It's thinking in advance about what it will feel like when friends start to have sex and talk about how great it is. Maybe the teen and his girlfriend need to agree that they'll make out to a certain point but then have some kind of signal that it's time to stop. For some teens, they need to tell their partner, "I'm very excited about going out with you, but I'm not going to have sex with you— I want to be clear about that." "It's like telling a waiter in a restaurant that you have an allergy to peanuts before they place your order," says Casparian. Using abstinence as a method of birth control takes the same amount of or even more planning as any other kind of method.

Helping your teenager imagine what it will be like to choose abstinence will not guarantee she'll stay a virgin through high school, but at least you will have helped her to plan and make careful choices rather than having sex "just happen" to her.

As awkward as this is, it's also a good idea to address the idea that yes, it is uncomfortable for a guy to get all worked up and not have an orgasm, but it is not harmful to him, despite what he may think or say. Parents of guys can tell them that using this as pressure to get a girl to go further than she is comfortable going can backfire if she feels regretful or angry about it afterward.

Many girls say that a very real concern is losing a guy because she won't have sex with him, followed closely by her fear of hurting his feelings by saying "no." It's not enough to simply tell your teen, "He's not worth it if he won't wait for you," because it's likely that she will not agree with that and will shut you out. Instead, talk about what *she* is worth, and ask her to turn the tables. Would she dump her boyfriend if he didn't want to do something that she was ready to do?

Talk the Talk: Teenagers Will Listen if You Say...

"What if someone wanted to have sex and you were not ready? How could you say no without hurting that person's feelings?"

"You're at the age now where you're starting to make more decisions for yourself, including very important decisions about sex—decisions that can have significant consequences such as STDs and unintended pregnancy. I'd like you to wait until [your goal here] before you have sex, but I realize that this is your choice, not mine. I want you to know that choosing *not* to have sex isn't something you just say; it's something you have to plan for in advance so you're not caught off guard in the moment. How can you set yourself up to succeed at your goal of abstaining to have sex until [your goal here]?"

Allow your teen to give a list of reasons and ideas so this isn't a monologue, and then you can add your own ideas. No matter what your morals or values are, help your teen understand that his feelings are important, and he has rights. You can even draw up a list of your teen's sexual rights.

A teen's bill of sexual rights:

• **You always have the right to say no to sex.** Even if you've said yes before, and even if you've "started something" that you don't want to finish.

• **It's okay for you to put your feelings first.** Your feelings matter.

• **You always have the right to choose** when, where, how, with whom, and *if* you are intimate.

• **You have the right to trust your judgment.** You are the final decision-maker when it comes to your body. When people want to get their way, they may say things to make you feel like you shouldn't trust your feelings or that your feelings don't matter.

• **You can put yourself first.** You are the most important person in your life. Look out for yourself.

HELP TEENS STAY SAFE

Eventually, every teenager is going to have sex. It might not be this year, it might not even be while he or she is a teenager. But it will happen. And when it does happen, it can be a good experience or a lousy experience or, worst-case scenario, an unwanted experience. As a parent (or mentor), you have the power to influence which it will be.

I listened when my parents said:

"Make sure it is really what you want. And don't be a fool; cover your tool."
                                                                    —Boy, 16, Ohio

A big part of planning for a positive experience is planning to prevent STDs and unintended pregnancy, which is covered in Chapter 9. Beyond that, talk to your teen about being sure she is making the right decision for her and not giving in to pressure to have sex. This is an important point for guys as well as girls. "There are guys who feel an enormous amount of pressure," says Casparian, "and they can't admit to their friends that they didn't enjoy it or that it wasn't fulfilling or that they feel bad after, or that they did it because they were pressured. It's hard for them to admit that to themselves."

You should also mention that alcohol and drugs make it more likely that he'll go further than he wanted to and less likely that he'll use birth control/STD-prevention tactics.

Susie Wilson, founder of the teen sexuality education website Sex, etc. says in Europe, "their whole society says: 'We're gong to teach you; we're going to make sure you get good services. We're not going to punish you, we don't want you to have a disease, we don't want you to have an unwanted pregnancy, we're going to talk to you about condoms, you're going to be able to get them,' all those things. And it's just more natural. If you talked to European teens, they have a much more healthy aspect about sex. Consequently, kids in Europe start having sex on average a whole year later than they do in the United States."

TIP: If you suspect your teen is sexually active but isn't admitting it to you, give her the information you feel she needs anyway (such as the birth control and pregnancy prevention information covered in Chapter 9). Don't wait.

You don't want your teen to think you don't know anything about sex or hormones, so it's a good idea to mention at some point that sex is pleasurable. You also don't want your teen to feel like "something's wrong" if he or she desires sex. Make it clear that it's perfectly normal for both boys and girls to fantasize about sex.

✳ Quick stat about regret: ✳

81% of sexually active young teens (age 12 to 14) wish they had waited longer to have sex.

—The National Campaign to Prevent Teen Pregnancy, 2003

Talk the Talk: Teenagers Will Listen if You Say...

"There's a reason people have sex—it feels good to be close to someone, when both partners are ready. But sex won't feel good, physically or emotionally, if you have it when you're not ready (like you feel pressured by your partner or you just get 'swept along' in the moment). It's also not the kind of thing where you want to be freaked out right after because you didn't take careful steps to protect against unwanted pregnancy and STDs. If you're at all thinking about having sex, now or in the future, it's important that you get the information you need to be safe and be sure it's a good experience, because I don't want you to regret it afterward. Can you think of something that might make you regret sex later? Can you think of a time when you might have sex and *not* regret it?"

"The first time you have sex will be something you'll always remember. So think about how you'll want to feel about the experience after—the day after, a week after and even years later. That's why, ideally, you don't want it to be something that 'just happens' at a party or with someone you're not close to. Do you think people think of losing their virginity as a big deal or something to 'get over with'? Which do you think it should be?"

"This is an awkward thing for me to say, but it's so important I'm going to say it anyway: I want you to promise me you won't fool around with someone when either you or the guy [or the girl] have been drinking. Just like I don't want you drinking and driving or riding in a car with anyone who's been drinking, this is just as dangerous, and the consequences can be just as severe."

continued

"You know I've said that I don't think sex is something that should 'just happen.' I want to bring it up again because I know you're getting to be an age where there might be alcohol at parties, and I want you to be careful. Obviously I would prefer that you not drink. But please hear me when I say that it's dangerous for you to drink alcohol at a party where there are boys because you'll be less able to make smart decisions and more likely to either make a decision you'll regret or, worst-case scenario, be taken advantage of by a boy who doesn't care about you (at least not at that moment). [For parents/mentors of boys: '. . . it's dangerous for you to drink alcohol at a party and then fool around with a girl. You might end up going further than you or she intended, and I know that it's far less likely that you'll be careful to protect against STDs/unwanted pregnancy. You also put yourself at risk if the girl decides the next day that she went farther than she wanted to and may even accuse you of pushing yourself on her. It's not worth the risk.'] What do you think you could say if you're at a party and everyone is drinking? Or if you're out on a date and the person brings alcohol? How can you get out of drinking without feeling uncool?"

This is also a good time to talk about how many drinks makes a person drunk and how girls get drunk more quickly than boys. Many teens who don't know this information end up drinking vast amounts of alcohol before realizing how intoxicated they've become, which can be dangerous for a whole host of reasons.

"I've noticed you have some new friends who are older, and I want to bring up the fact that older friends might be ready for things that you might not be ready for, like having sex. It's easier to feel like 'everyone is doing it' when your friends are older and maybe more of them are, but I want you to please be sure that you make decisions that are right for you. Can you think of a time when everyone around you was doing something and you thought it was the wrong thing? You don't even have to tell me what it was—just remember that feeling . . . "

"You need to live with your choices long after you've moved away from these friends or gone to college or your separate ways or whatever. Try to make important decisions by thinking about what you alone want to do and are comfortable with. I will always be here for you, but in the end you are the only one who will need to live with the choices you make. Because of this, I want you to be in control, and not to give up control of this (or any) big decision to your boyfriend [or girlfriend] or your friends or me or anyone else."

Finally, you of course want to help your teen avoid any kind of unwanted sex. Again, about 1 in 10 sexually active girls under the age of 15 report that their first sexual experience was "nonvoluntary." This does not mean all those girls were raped by strangers. But you would never want your teenager to feel he or she was coerced, manipulated, or forced into having sex. You can copy these "stay-safe" rules and hand them to your teen so she can study them on her own, but follow up to be sure she's read them. (Even if you have to play a little "how to stay safe" *Jeopardy!*–style game at the breakfast table, it's worth it to be sure your teen has internalized this information.)

Please take some steps to always stay safe:

• **Trust your instincts.** If you feel scared, something's probably wrong. Get away and/or call me right away. Even if you end up feeling foolish, that's better than not acting on your feelings and finding out later that you were right to be scared.

• **If you ever feel threatened or unsafe you can always call me** and I will come get you, no questions asked and no preaching. Use a code word, like call me [a special name here] and I'll know that means "Come get me now."

- Even if you've known your date for a while, **never let anyone get you alone**. Always stay within earshot of other people.

- **Speak clearly and firmly** about your limits so your date doesn't think you mean "If you push me more, I might say yes."

- **Drinking or doing drugs makes you vulnerable.**

- **Never drink anything that wasn't opened in front of you.**

- **Don't be afraid to call 911** if you are afraid.

- **Never feel like you "owe"** anyone sex or sexual favors.

- **If something bad ever happens to you:**
  1. Get to a safe place as fast as you can.
  2. Call 911.
  3. Call me and I'll come to you right away.
  4. Don't wash up or use the bathroom.
  5. We'll get you to a hospital right away.

I hope you never need this information, but I want you to have it.
Your safety is the most important thing to me.
I want you to take every step possible to protect yourself,
but please know that
I will never blame you
if someone forces you to do something you don't want to do.

TIP: Explain to your teenager what "no means no" means. Give some examples and ideas for what to do or say if they're not clear on how far their partner wants to go.

THE LAST WORD

In the end, the most important message you can give a teenager about virginity is that it is your sincere hope that their first time will be a safe and positive experience. You feel it's an important decision, and you're always willing to talk about it or answer questions about it. However, this one moment in time does not define him or her. It is one aspect of the complex history that will help shape the adult they ultimately turn out to be.

The **Media** Can Actually Be a Good Influence

* **Exclusive National Survey Results** *
Teens: Tell the Truth!

Where do you get most of your information about sex?

> **My Parents 38%**
>
> **Friends 23%**
>
> **School/Sex Ed. 22%**
>
> **TV 3%**
>
> **Older Sibling 4%**
>
> **The Internet 2%**
>
> **My boyfriend/girlfriend 1%**
>
> **Other/don't know 7%**

*

**Young people (ages 8 to 18) devote almost 6½ hours a day
to recreational media**
—Kaiser Family Foundation, 2005

When people say "sex is everywhere," what they really mean is, "It's on TV, which is in my living room, which makes me feel like I'm living in a sexually charged world and my child is being barraged with messages saying that sex is fun and consequence-free, and . . . help!"

The average American teenager watches over three hours of TV a day and spends more than an hour a day online. No teen will ever say that they saw something on TV or in a movie and then ran out to copy it, though teens will admit that on TV and in the movies (and in a different way, on the Internet) sex is made to look pretty casual and carefree. There have been steps taken to change this. The Kaiser Family Foundation reported in 2003 that of the 1,100 shows with sexual content in the previous season, 26 percent of those that depicted or talked about sexual intercourse made some mention of safer sex, nearly double the number when they did the study 4 years previously. But also going up is the number of shows with sexual content— reported to be two-thirds of all shows; and four-fifths of shows that are commonly watched by teens.

If you pick a teen or a preteen out of a crowd, I can guarantee he or she has seen *Friends* (or whatever the new version of *Friends* is), probably *American Pie,* and all kinds of sites on the Internet that we don't even know about. As someone who's had many occasions to Internet-search for "teens and sex," you don't want to know some of the stuff that's come up on my screen. So teens are exposed to sex in the media, and plenty of it. This doesn't necessarily have to be a bad or dangerous thing, but of course no one wants teenagers getting their formative ideas about sex and romance (or really, anything important in life) from TV, the movies, or the Internet.

But shielding teenagers them from these messages won't work. If you say they can't watch a certain show because it's too sexy or a movie because it's rated R or play a certain video game, they'll just go to a friend's house and check it out anyway because they are curious, and if "everyone else" is watching/seeing/playing that game, they're going to want to know why. "Sometimes parents think they've lost their teens to popular culture," says Marisa Nightingale, senior director of media programs and youth initiatives at The National Campaign to Prevent Teen Pregnancy "But the media is not this *thing* that's taken over teens; it's actually a tool that parents can use to their advantage." Besides, with two-thirds of all programming (excluding children's shows, news, and sports) containing sexual content, you'd have to pretty much banish the TV altogether.

But many parents underestimate how much guidance preteens and teens still need as consumers of media. This isn't about censorship, but it is important that parents serve as a kind of filter to help teens interpret and even reject some of the messages they get from mass media. The media is not your enemy—actually it is your helper as you open doors of communication with your teen. But there are definitely media realities that you should be aware of.

SEX ON TV AFFECTS TEENS' BEHAVIOR

At the time of this writing, a new study by Rand Corporation showed a correlation between teens who watch a lot of sex on TV and teens who have sex at a younger age. And this wasn't talking about R-rated movies. The study found that shows that talk a lot about sex or have a lot of sexual innuendo have just as much of an impact as those that show sex. Of course, this came as no major surprise to anyone; obviously TV influences our behavior, or else advertisers wouldn't spend so much money promoting products via commercials.

One reaction to this news was fairly predictable: a legion of people denounced Hollywood and TV producers and demanded that networks show more "family-friendly" fare during the "family hour," which apparently, is 8 to 9 P.M. (Is it funny that "family hour" means watching TV as a family?) The trouble with trying to censor the networks, of course, is who gets to decide what's "family friendly"? And besides, hasn't the horse really left the barn here? *Friends* has been on TV for 10 years. If you have a teen, he's seen it and has probably noticed, as one *USA Today* columnist who read a few hundred plot synopses of *Friends* pointed out, that Rachel had around 20 different sex partners over the course of the series, 5 of which were in the context of relationships.

"You can get entire lessons on sex . . . in one episode"

"People think that teens are too young to know anything about sex. Well I think differently. Just by watching popular shows such as *Friends* and *Sex and the City,* you can get entire lessons on sex in one episode. Pop culture is full of lessons on sex, and if you absorb enough information you can easily put two and two together. I didn't know what a pearl necklace was until I watched an episode of *Sex and the City.* Nor did I know what tea-bagging was until I watched the movie *Soul Plane.* Now everyone who has seen *Soul Plane* at my school knows what it is and most are only 14 and 15, some younger than that. Luckily though I am one of the few kids I know with a mother who isn't uptight about sex because she has taken the time to explain how it works. Now I am no longer so susceptible to the myths some of my friends believe in."

—Lina, 15, Colorado

"They figured out that sex sells"

"I think there's nothing that can really stop it. Basically they figured out that sex sells so they publicize it on TV. And when you're watching stuff like music videos, you see great looking girls and great looking guys and people out there that dress skimpy and stuff like that. It opens people up to sex a lot younger than a lot of people think they should be opened up to it. It's everywhere, Music . . . all these little guys and girls see the music videos, it's obviously opened up by that. I'm one to think it's stupid to talk about how people killed themselves because a musical artist promoted it, but sexual-wise, it definitely opens up through pop music."

—Jake, 15, Missouri

But many teens also say they have learned something helpful about sexual decision making from TV. A 2002 Kaiser study showed that almost half (43 percent) of teens say TV has taught them how to talk with a partner about safer sex, and 6 in 10 say they have learned from TV how to say no to a sexual situation that makes them uncomfortable.

✳ *How much TV do teens watch?* ✳

Over 3 hours a day   —Kaiser Family Foundation, 2005

As far as TV or movies being a bad influence, though, it seems unlikely that teens, who tend to be much smarter than we give them credit for, are going to watch one sitcom episode and then be inspired to run off and have unprotected sex. But getting the same message over and over, whether it's "you must be rich and thin to be happy" or "sex is fun and carries no consequences," is bound to have an influence on anyone's psyche. The good news is that teenagers can handle these messages on TV, as well as in movies, in music, and on the Internet. They are capable of sorting through them and still being moral individuals who make smart choices. The other news is that to do this, they'll need your help.

TIP: A mother of teen boys recommends screenit.com, a site that gives details about how violent or sexually graphic a movie is. You have to buy a subscription but, as the mom put it, "this site tells you exactly what swear words are used, what sex acts are shown—it's almost more than you want to know."

THERE'S HARD-CORE PORNOGRAPHY IN THE SCHOOL LIBRARY

Friends is one thing. But a surprising number of teens report, rather nonchalantly, that they check out pornography on the Internet and in fact, often do so using their school library's computer. Here's what one 15-year-old from Cleveland had to say about this:

"Guys at my school looked at porn"

"Guys from my school looked at porn. They did it because, well I guess they have nothing better to do, and their parents never found out. So they probably thought 'Why not?' It does influence their behavior; what respect they had for girls before, it is now totally gone. All they would think about or talk about was sex or sex-oriented stuff. Like the guys just look at girls and think: 'Oh, she would be a good porn star.' And I know this because I have heard the guys rating the girls as 'she would make a good porn star' or 'she wouldn't.'

"Some of the guys I know try to pressure girls into doing stuff they don't want to do. But the girls are smart enough to say no or walk away—most of them at least."   —Lisa, 15, Ohio

Pornography does often, as this teen points out, portray women as sexual objects. And if boys are not exposed to other, positive messages about sex and relationships, or if their first erotic experience is looking at hard-core pornography, they can easily develop a warped sense of what sex and love look and feel like.

✳ Who's seeing online pornography? ✳

Among all online youth age 15 to 17,
70% say they have accidentally stumbled
across pornography online.
41% of 15- to 17-year-olds say such exposure is "no big deal."
—Kaiser Family Foundation, 2001

Yet many teens talk about Internet porn casually, as if it's just another facet of life that they deal with regularly. "I don't go into chat rooms, ever," says Davie, 17, from Chicago. "The Internet is available at my school, and I've seen some people look at porn online." And Edgar, 15, from Missouri, says, "I try to stay away from Internet porn. It is degrading to the women and to think that that girl is someone's little girl, and I looked at her like that and I didn't even know who she was—it affected me. And it's just gross and sick of the guys. It does change the way I look at girls . . . but not a lot."

When it is widely reported that certain celebrities have had sex flicks circulating on the Internet, perhaps it's inevitable that porn has become so "normalized" that some teens have even filmed homemade porn movies.

Several prestigious private schools have recently been struck by such scandals. In some cases, it was unclear which of the participants knew the tapes would be so widely viewed.

I listened when my parents said:

"Tell the truth, and no one can catch you in a lie."

—Boy, 16, South Carolina

TEENS ARE INTERNET DATING

This probably comes as no shock because teens love to go online and chat and make connections with teens they know, and many teens also like to make new friends online. A 2002 Kaiser report showed that 95 percent of teens have accessed the Internet; by now it's probably closer to 100 percent. We all know about dating services and friend-making sites where teens are not supposed to go (because these sites are supposed to be for adults), but they often do anyway. The same report noted that 1 in 4 boys age 15 to 17 had lied about their age to access a website. In addition to these "meet new people" sites, a lot of sites aren't specifically intended to be dating sites but they do encourage users to build a profile that can include details about yourself physically, your likes and dislikes—even a photo. Teens may not realize this, but any site that allows users to build a profile and see other user's profiles is going to draw some people who are looking to date. That's how this teen started a relationship with a much older guy:

"We fell in love ... online"

"I'm 16 and I have a secret, because of the kind of family and friends I have, I couldn't tell anyone. But I'm more than willing to tell you ... I must admit, I do talk to a lot of people on the Internet. And well, I've been meeting some really nice guys and everything. Well this one guy I met, he was just a dream come true: respectful, considerate, honest, talkative, the list goes on. But he was 22 and I'm only 16. We exchanged e-mails as well as phone conversations. Then we decided that we should take our friendship to the next level and become a couple.

"We began to fall deeper and deeper in love. Until one day, he proposed to me. And I said yes. We even started calling ourselves 'Mr. and Mrs. [his last name].' But on the day after our 3-week anniversary, I received an e-mail from a young lady saying *she* also was his girlfriend and that they had been dating for a month and a half. This broke my heart completely. So I wrote him an e-mail and broke it all off.

"It's been a month, and I still wake up at night crying and I think about him all the time. And the truth is, if I didn't respect myself as much as I do, I'd call him right now, and take him back ... because I still love him."

—Cecilia, 16, Virginia

Internet dating for teens isn't just unwise; it can be extremely unsafe. Cecilia did not give this guy her home address or phone number, but other, less savvy teens have not been so lucky. In September 2004, a 13-year-old girl befriended someone on the Internet who she thought was also a teenager. It turned out he was a pedophile who managed to lure her to his apartment where she was held captive for days. This is one of those issues that is so important it's worth it to talk about it several times—Internet technology has allowed teenagers to be smarter and learn a lot of amazing, exciting things, but it's also a gateway for strangers to come into your home and court them, just when they're most vulnerable and open to love and attention.

With all that is risky for teens on the Internet, should you spy on their Internet behavior to see what they're getting into?

Parents Speak Out:
"I read my teen's AIM messages"

"I did once stoop to the level of infiltrating my son's AIM messages—they sometimes keep logs, which is something I found out by mistake. I don't know how much is true and what he and his friends are just saying to be cool, but I caught my son talking about things I didn't know he was into. Maybe it's not the best way to get information, but I was concerned. I think the test is: are you doing it to protect them, or because you're curious? I'll admit that I was curious and did read more than I needed to, so I just stopped, cold turkey. But if you're doing it to keep your kid safe, I think it's okay. Keeping them safe is more important than sacrificing a little bit of their privacy, I think."   —Wisconsin mother of two teen boys

This question poses the same moral dilemma as reading a teen's diary or journal. The mom quoted above admitted to me that she became addicted to reading her teen's instant messages to the degree that she'd rush home from work to see what he'd been talking about that day, as if it were a soap opera. Unless it's a real emergency where you're concerned for your teen's health or safety, it's best to avoid this kind of privacy-invading measure. When and if the teen catches you, he'll feel it's the ultimate invasion of privacy and may keep other, important information from you as punishment. A better idea is to initiate conversations about what they're doing on the Internet and ask your teen about the AIMs he sends and receives. He may even show them to you willingly if you ask.

REAL-WORLD ADVICE

It's a little overwhelming to realize the kinds of messages teens have coming at them from so many different angles, but remember that you have the power to help them interpret those messages. Your teen is looking to you to help her create her values. (Ever notice, for example, how when your teen talks about politics with friends, her ideas closely mimic yours?) No matter how powerful you feel the media is, *you* are the primary influence on your teens when it comes to sex and sexual decision making.

One thing teens hate is feeling manipulated. You can use this to your advantage by helping your teen see and sidestep the degree of manipulation the media attempts to use. Start here:

WATCH WHAT THEY'RE WATCHING

Ask your teen what she's watching, listening to, and where she goes on the Internet. She may be totally honest with you and will probably assume that you won't check out these CDs, movies, TV shows, and websites she's naming. But she's wrong—because there's an enormous value to your checking out the media she's absorbing. You will get an insider's view of what she's feeling, seeing, and thinking about. And what you see may surprise you.

The movie that kept coming up over and over in my interviews was *American Pie*. It's often aired on cable and is rentable on DVD, and everyone I've interviewed has seen it. Except parents. Almost no parents have seen *American Pie*. I can understand why parents would take a pass on this one, but I'd urge you to watch it (or whatever is the new teen sexcapade movie these days)—to really see what teens are seeing. Get in the loop, so you can talk about these movies from a place of knowledge. Today's teen sex comedies are not much more raunchy than they were 10 or 15 years ago, but it's easy to forget just how explicit they are until you actually see one.

✳ How TV influences teens ✳

**65% of teens who viewed a particular episode
of *Friends* recalled that show's specific information about
condom-efficacy rates.
As a result of watching the episode, 10% of teen viewers talked with a
parent or another adult about the effectiveness of condoms.**
—RAND, 2004

Books aimed at teens also give graphic depictions of teen life. You don't have to form a book club with your teen (though that can be fun and a good way to get conversations going), but be aware of what books she's reading. You might also find it enlightening to read them yourself. Ask her what she liked about the book and whether she felt like the situations and the characters' reactions were "real" or seemed fake. You'll get an idea of how she's thinking and feeling about situations that you might not otherwise talk about. If you have a teen boy, you might notice that he's looking at some of those so-called "laddie" magazines that are aimed at adult men, but teen guys certainly read them. Leaf through one and see what kind of language they're using to describe sex and relationships, as well as how women are portrayed.

The same goes for the Internet: find out what sites he likes to visit and check them out. Ask him questions about the content, and try to understand why he likes that site, what he's getting out of it. Many boys like game sites, whereas girls tend to gravitate toward sites where they can connect with other people. "Go into their world and see what your child is exposed to—watch their favorite reality shows, go into the mall and look at what the mannequins are wearing," advises Laura Gauld, director of family education at the Hyde Schools (New England–based boarding schools that focus on character development). Read their magazines, listen to their music . . . it'll all help you get inside your teen's head and help to open up a new kind of dialogue between the two of you.

✳ The media gets teens and parents talking ✳

42% of teens say that in the past year or so, something in the
media sparked a conversation with their friends or parents about the
consequences of sex.
72% of teens' parents say they had such a conversation
with their children or friends because of something they
saw in the media.
Most adults and teens (84% and 82% respectively) wish
the media showed more about the consequences of sex,
including teen pregnancy.

—The National Campaign to Prevent Teen Pregnancy, 2004

TIP: If your teen likes to IM, send him an IM (or a text message on his cell phone) every now and again. He may bring up topics with you over IM that he'd be too embarrassed to bring up in person.

WATCH WHAT THEY'RE WATCHING WITH THEM

One parent told me about her 13-year-old son, who insisted that every single one of his friends was allowed to watch *Sex and the City* and they all talked about it at school the next day and he was completely left out because he wasn't allowed to see it. So she said, "Fine, you can watch it . . . *I'll watch it with you.*" It's not easy to see people making out or simulating full-blown intercourse with your teen in the room, but it does give you the opportunity to provide a running commentary: "It's interesting that they're not showing birth control, but obviously they're using it since no one is ending up pregnant or with STDs." Even if he rolls his eyes or shhhhs you, you can rest assured he's hearing what you say.

Talk the Talk: Teenagers Will Listen if You Say…

"I saw *American Pie*—the pie scene, whoa. Let me ask you: how realistic do you think that movie was? Do people really have bets about when they'll lose their virginity? Do a lot of people have sex on prom night? Why do you think prom is a time people might choose to have sex? If you were going to go to prom and didn't want to have sex or didn't feel ready to, what could you say to your date before the prom so you didn't get into a situation? What could you do the night of the prom to avoid feeling really uncomfortable if your date was expecting sex?"

"I glanced through your magazine today and noticed the kissing lessons. Do you think a lot of people your age are kissing—real kissing like in that article? Do people kiss someone who's their boyfriend/girlfriend or someone they met at a party or what? Hmm, interesting. Listen, even though it doesn't seem like a big deal, kissing is intimate and I think people should kiss once they know each other enough to feel close and to feel respect for each other. I know a lot of people may not agree with me and may feel comfortable kissing someone they met at a party or something, but for some people, kissing can feel serious, so just keep that in mind, okay?"

"We often slam media," says Jennifer Oliphant, community outreach coordinator for The National Teen Pregnancy Prevention Research Center at the University of Minnesota, "but it can also be an opportunity to feel out a kid and find out where they are in their understanding." Oliphant describes an eye-opening moment that occurred when she was teaching health education to a class of fourth graders. She asked them about what they'd seen on TV about sex. One girl started describing a scene she had watched, and it became apparent that she was talking about having seen oral sex in a pornographic movie. Even though that's obviously an extreme example, teenagers are seeing a lot of sex, both graphic and implied, so even if you have a much more mundane example, you can use it as a springboard for discussion.

TALK TO YOUR TEEN ABOUT SAFE INTERNET USE

When teens need information these days, they don't just wring their hands. They'll often ask their friends, who can be a good source of information—or misinformation. Girls tend to get a lot of information from magazines (both teen magazines and magazines intended for adults), and boys and girls are also accustomed to doing their research online. "I think that one of the trends today is the fact that teens are bypassing adults," says Susie Wilson, founder of Sex, Etc. Half of 15- to 17-year-olds use the Internet to find the answers to their sexual health questions, so it's worth it to point your teen to some sites that you feel have reliable information.

TIP: Some sites to explore: www.goaskalice.columbia.edu, sxetc.org, teenwire.com, teenpregnancy.org.

Always check out a site yourself to be sure you're comfortable with the degree of information and candor it provides. If the site has a Q&A section, look up questions you think your teen may have, and see if you're comfortable with the answers given.

If teens stick to sites you've approved, chances are they won't be bombarded with explicit pop-ups while they're trying to get answers to their questions—but it's no guarantee. One mom I spoke to told me she once looked over her shoulder at her son's screen and was appalled at the sexy pop-ups that were boing-ing up on his screen. She told him she was sure he was being targeted because he'd visited a questionable site. Then the same thing started happening to *her*. "I realized this can just happen to anyone," she says, a tad sheepishly. And have you ever gotten an e-mail sent to you at work with a horrific subject line? That can happen to teens as well. It's worth it to look into the pop-up blocker and spam-prevention software that's available—it's not perfect, but it can shield your teenager from some of the unsavory stuff out there.

TIP: Consider implementing the "parental controls" on your teen's IM account so she can only send and receive IMs from people she knows.

If you have a teenager who's using the Internet, it's also vital that you reiterate the safety rules of web use—you may even want to write them down on a sticky note and put them next to the computer:

Rules for Safe Internet Use

- **Never give out any personal information online, including:**

  - **Your full name**

  - **Address**

  - **Where your parents work**

  - **Phone number**

  - **Photograph**

  - **Personal e-mail address**

  - **Social Security number or any other ID numbers (school, driver's license, etc.)**

- **Be sure your screen name and e-mail address are very different from your real name.**

- **Never, ever agree to meet any online friends in person unless you set up a meeting that includes your parents and the other teen's parents.**

- **Keep your guard up. Many people lie online about how old they are or where they live or why they are interested in you.**

Don't just tell your teenager how dangerous this can be; give specific examples of things you've read about in the papers or heard on the news. When teens feel like you're overreacting or saying something "just because," they'll tune out, and this is an especially important message for them to tune into.

TIP: If something is very important, ask your teen to make you a promise about it. You can't overdo this or it loses its power, but many teens report to me that they are loath to break a promise they've made to their parents.

If you troll teen sites, you'll notice that it doesn't take long for someone to suggest "phone sex," which is sometimes conducted in chat rooms or via instant message. Take this comment, which I saw on a mainstream teen chat room recently: "I'm bored. N E 1 up for phone sex? If Yes press 123 and I will IM U."

TIP: For more information about online safety for teens, check out safeteens.com.

When talking to your teen about safety and the Internet, you should also bring up the fact that sexual pressure occurs online as well, and that Internet "fooling around" can have emotional consequences, especially if he or she starts to feel a bond with someone they only know via the Internet. (This can easily happen—who wouldn't want to get "love letters" every day?) Because you have no way of verifying the other person's identity, it's best to keep Internet friends just that.

Talk the Talk: Teenagers Will Listen if You Say...

"You know, I was doing some Internet research today, and all of a sudden a pop-up ad came up for a porn site. I don't know if you've ever seen porn, but it seems like if you use the Internet it can be kind of shoved at you, like it was at me. And I can understand if you're curious about it—it's hard not to be. But I want you to know that I'd rather you not look at pornography, because I don't like the way women are generally portrayed in porn. Also the sex in pornography isn't loving and it often isn't protected, and I just think it kind of makes sex into something that's graphic and ugly instead of a caring, intimate act between people who love each other, which is how I think sex should be."

"I was on a site today and I noticed that you can build a profile of your likes and dislikes and all that. You know a lot of people will look at those profiles as kind of a dating service, so I feel strongly that you not build a profile and that you never give out your name, photo, address, phone number, or even your e-mail address to anyone online."

"There have been lots of cases where people pose as teenagers, and they can be very convincing. I never want you to get into a dangerous situation so I need you to promise me that you'll never meet in person anyone you met online unless you talk to me about it first and I go with you. I know it sounds extreme, but I care about you so much that I simply can't risk someone hurting you—and it's happened. [If your teen seems unconvinced, tell the story of the kidnapped teen here.] If someone asks you for your real name or address, how can you say no in a way that won't hurt their feelings? What other kinds of personal information might someone ask you for if they're trying to figure out who you are or where you live?"

TIP: If you see something that looks at all like child pornography or solicitation, report it to your local FBI office (find it at: www.fbi.gov/contact/fo/fo.htm) and call the child pornography tip line at 800-843-5678.

TEACH YOUR TEEN HOW TO INTERPRET MESSAGES IN THE MEDIA

The next time you're watching TV with your teenager, especially if he's a younger teen, when an ad comes on showing, say, a ripped, virile guy applying shaving lotion while girls smile at him from outside his bathroom window, start a discussion about it. Ask him what he thinks the shaving cream manufacturer is trying to say about what happens when you use their lotion. You'll get him thinking about the ways advertisers use television as a medium to influence the way people think and about the messages behind the message.

TIP: Try to have talks about sex and dating when you're one-on-one with your teen. If you and your spouse or partner approach your teen together, she can feel ganged-up-on and be less likely to speak openly and truthfully.

You can use this same technique with video games or TV shows or even movies. Ask him to be an analytical viewer and not just a passive receiver of media. "The way women are portrayed in many T-rated video games is generally very sexualized," says Harvard associate professor Kimberly Thompson, D.Sc., lead author on the study *Violence in Teen-Rated Video Games.* "We found sexual material and themes in a significant percentage of the teen-rated games," she adds. Thompson talked about a skater video game she studied that's very popular right now. The female character, she notes, is based on a porn star and even has some pithy comments in the "extras" along the lines of "Get ready for X . . . X . . . X . . . TREME action!!"

It seems like the easy thing to do when you make a discovery like this is to forbid the playing of the game. But that's not a real solution, because you're imposing your standards on your teenager instead of empowering him to make his own smart choices. As soon as you make a rule, as soon as you dismiss his desire to play the game by saying something like "Oh, this is obscene. This is not acceptable. You can't play it . . ." you're making it seem like you don't think your teenager is capable of coming to an intelligent conclusion on his own. Dictating makes teens tune out and assume you don't "get it."

When you empower teens, however, they feel trusted to be responsible and make good decisions. You're helping your teen become a critical consumer, instead of a passive consumer, of mass culture, because you can't always be with him when it's time for him to make these decisions. And know that teens tend to get annoyed whenever they feel people are trying to manipulate them. They hate it. All you have to do is give a little nudge and expose the manipulation. They might even rebel against it by not patronizing that particular brand or product.

Talk the Talk: Teenagers Will Listen if You Say...

"Isn't the technology in this game amazing? It's incredible to me how real the characters look and all the moves they can do. Did you know—don't you think it's kind of surprising that this character is actually based on a pornography star? Why do you think the makers of this game would do that?"

THE LAST WORD

Instead of fighting against the media, use it to start a conversation. Just by showing you're interested enough in your teenager to explore his favorite music, movies, websites, TV shows, and video games, you're sending the message that you care enough to really invest the time to get to know what's important to him. It's this kind of deeper-level connecting that will make your teen that much more likely to want to listen to you and keep the lines of communication open.

Sex Ed. Is Not at All Like It Used to Be

61.6% of 12th graders have had sex.

—CDC Youth Risk Behavior Surveillance Survey, 2003

*

* **Exclusive National Survey Results** *
Teens: Tell the Truth!

52% of 17-year-olds say that someone has taught them how to use a condom correctly.

*

13% of teens believe they are getting enough information about abstinence and contraception.

—The National Campaign to Prevent Teen Pregnancy, 2003

"People should stress in sex education what can happen to you. Because people have sex without thinking."   —Maxon, 16, Missouri

Many parents view sex ed. as a "get-out-of-talking-about-sex-free-card." But in actuality, this class, which is often offered as "health" and in some districts is taught every year from fifth grade on, provides another great opportunity to have meaningful discussions with your teenager on the topic. You probably know that not all sex ed. classes are created equal, but you may not know that parents and other concerned members of your community can have a profound influence on what is taught in your local school (see "Real-World Advice," later in this chapter, for some suggestions on how to do this). Some private schools or religious schools may not have sex ed. at all. In public schools, how sexual health and sexuality information is presented to young people and who presents it can vary widely from state to state and even from school to school.

Many states have some legal restrictions about what must and what cannot be taught in sex education classes. It's a very political issue, as you have likely read in the papers. If you're not sure about the laws governing what's taught in sex education classes in your state, you can find out by going to www.siecus.org/policy/states.

There are two basic schools of thought in sex education. Advocacy groups on both sides of this issue have different names for each of these theories, but they boil down to abstinence-only sex education and comprehensive (or "abstinence-plus") sex education. In both kinds of sex ed. students are usually taught how their bodies work and how pregnancy happens. They may also be taught about STDs, including HIV, and sometimes other topics such as relationships, sexual pressure, morals, sexual ethics, and rape may be covered.

The main difference is that in abstinence-only sex ed. students are not taught about birth control or STD prevention, and condoms or other contraceptives may only be mentioned in terms of failure rates. Comprehensive (abstinence-plus) sex education stresses abstinence as the first-choice form of birth control and STD prevention, and also provides students with an overview of how birth control and various STD-prevention methods work.

✳ What kind of sex ed. do parents want? ✳

67 percent believe federal funding should support comprehensive
programs that include information on how to obtain and use
condoms and other contraceptives.
51 percent believe sex ed. should provide information and guidance
to help teens make their own decisions.
30 percent believe federal funding should support
abstinence-only programs.
—Kaiser Family Foundation/Kennedy School of Government, 2003

Research has proven that teaching students about contraception does not hasten sexual activity, nor does it give teens a mixed message. More data is expected in 2005, and still more research is needed to figure out exactly how best to present different messages to teens to make the greatest impression upon them.

TIP: Call your teen's school and request a copy of your child's sex ed. curriculum so you know exactly what is (and is not) being taught.

Sex education is valuable and necessary. Ideally, there would be a way to integrate the two schools of thought and get everyone on board with a curriculum that would accomplish everyone's common goal: preparing teens to act safely and responsibly. As Sarah Brown, director of The National Campaign to Prevent Teen Pregnancy, often says about this political debate: "While adults argue, teens get pregnant." Teens need information from a reliable, credible source in order to find that information helpful. Sex ed. gives us an opportunity to provide that source, while also sending the unified message that as a society, we are not okay with teens getting pregnant or contracting STDs.

WHEN TEENS NEED INFORMATION,
THEY TRY TO FIND IT

Keep in mind that teens often fill in the blanks incorrectly when they're given unclear or incomplete information. If you don't make sure your teen knows the mechanics of how she can get pregnant (or how he can get a girl pregnant), all the teen has to go on is what her friends tell her, or what she reads on the Internet.

This may account for the many myths that even some sophisticated teens believe. For example: "If you douche with cola after sex, you can't get pregnant" is one that Jeanne Stanley, director, Bryson Institute of the Attic Youth Center, has heard a bunch of times. When I was sex and body editor at *Seventeen* I got a letter from a girl asking if she could get "pregnate" by washing her underwear with her father's. Go to any teen advice site and look at the questions teens are asking to get a load of other myths floating around these days.

The less solid information teens get, the more they are likely to make stuff up on their own. This is even more unsettling when you consider that studies show, Dr. Blum (who in addition to being chairman of the Department of Population and Family Health Sciences at the Johns Hopkins Bloomberg School of Public Health is also director of the World Health Organization's Collaborating Center on Adolescent Health) says, that "most moms don't ever talk to their kids about contraception, plain and simply—probably two thirds to three quarters don't ever discuss it." And when young people have incorrect beliefs about how to prevent pregnancy or STDs, bad things can happen.

"There's nowhere else in our educational system, in my opinion, where we say, Okay, we're gong to learn algebra, but I'm not going to give you any of the theorems," says Jennifer Oliphant, community outreach coordinator for the National Teen Pregnancy Prevention Research Center at the University of Minnesota. When teens need answers, Oliphant points out, they look them up on the Internet and go to their friends. They'll go anywhere they can, really, to try to uncover the truth.

Teens echo this feeling. As Cathleen, 15, from Missouri puts it: "I always go to my best friend for advice about sex stuff, but I know that she's feeling the same way I am. She's just my age, and she's just as stupid, so she's not always giving me the best advice. But sometimes, it's kind of lame, but sometimes I go to forums online where there's adults who can give you advice—just someone who doesn't know who I am. I wish I had an older sister who had already gone through things I have who I could talk to. It would be a lot easier."

SEX ED. CLASSES VARY WIDELY

In sex ed. classes across the country, there's a wide range of what and how teens are taught about sex and sexual health. More than a handful of teens told me that in their sex ed. class, they were shown large, blown-up pictures of "STDs gone wild" and were convinced that sex could lead to horrific illness and should, in fact, be avoided. Other teens say there is very little talk of actual sex in their sex ed. class at all.

TIP: Review, then offer your teen a list of sites with correct, scientific information, such as teenwire.com, sxetc.org, or teenpregnancy.org.

HOW CAN SEX ED. BE MOST HELPFUL TO STUDENTS?

Most experts I speak to, and in fact most teenagers themselves, believe that most teens are better off waiting until after high school to start having sex. As young adults, they're developmentally better able to plan into the future, to anticipate consequences, and to take steps to protect against unwanted pregnancy and STDs.

However, in sex as in life, teenagers often do not act the way adults want them to. More than 60 percent of high school seniors have had sex. In 2004, researchers from Columbia and Yale determined that though virginity pledges seem to encourage teens to delay sex, 88 percent of teens who pledge not to have sex before marriage end up breaking that pledge. So even teens who have discussed abstinence with people who care about them and made a concerted effort can have a hard time, ultimately, keeping that promise.

"We know that—after emphasizing that abstinence is the best approach—talking about condoms and contraception, and even making contraception available, does not increase sexual behavior," says Douglas Kirby, Ph.D., senior research scientist with ETR Associates, a health education organization in California. This is confirmed by many studies, including Kirby's "Emerging Answers: Research Findings on Programs to Reduce Teen Pregnancy" and an in-depth study by the Joint United Nations Programme on HIV/AIDS.

But is it confusing to teens to say, "Don't have sex, but if you do, use a condom"? It turns out that teens seem to be able to decipher this message. The National Campaign to Prevent Teen Pregnancy, a nonprofit, nonpartisan organization dedicated to reducing teen pregnancy in the United States, surveyed teens and parents to ask if stressing abstinence while providing information about birth control was a "mixed message." They found that 77 percent of teens felt this was in fact a "clear and specific message."

There are entire books written on this topic, and people dedicate their lives to advocating for various forms of sex education, so I'm not going to go any further into the politics here. No matter what a person's individual beliefs are, any time a parent helps their teen understand those beliefs and takes steps to ensure that the teen is acting safely and responsibly and from a place of knowledge and wisdom, that parent is giving their child a meaningful gift. What all sides agree on is that teens need to feel that the topic is not taboo at home, so they don't go on an information quest from various sources of dubious reliability. "Parents, you are the primary sex educator of your child," says Leslee Unruh, founder of the Abstinence Clearinghouse.

The most recent CDC data analyzing the reasons for the decline in teen pregnancy revealed that about half of the decline is due to increased use of contraception, and about half is due to teens abstaining from sex. "Everybody's right," says Sarah Brown, director of The National Campaign to Prevent Teen Pregnancy. "Teen pregnancy rates are going down in every state in the nation and every ethnic group. There's no single corner on wisdom here. School-based education and services are helping, and we have evidence that parent-child communication helps, youth development helps, after-school programs can help. Whatever we are all doing, we need to keep doing it."

✳ What do teens want to be taught? ✳

**81% of teens wish they were getting more information
about abstinence and contraception rather than just one or
the other.
68% of adults view a message that stresses abstinence while also
providing information about contraception as
"clear and specific."
Two thirds of teens feel this message does not encourage teens
to have sex.**
—The National Campaign to Prevent Teen Pregnancy, 2004

Parents are a very important part of this equation. Relying on school as a teen's only (or even primary) source of sex ed. information can be dangerous, because even under the best circumstances, where the class is fantastic and covers all the topics a parent would want, it's impossible to guarantee that all the teens in the class pay close attention every single day, attend every class, and never tune out during crucial points.

WHAT TEENS HAVE TO SAY ABOUT SEX ED.

Perhaps because sex ed. is an inherently embarrassing topic, many students tell me they think their class is "stupid" or "a joke." Many times they say they "already know everything" that's being taught in sex education classes.

"Nowadays, kids know everything"

"We had sex ed. in school. Just like basically, all they teach you is stuff you already know. They teach you all about STDs and to use protection, and how to use protection. Nowadays, kids know everything, so I think that's part of the reason why everything moves faster now. I think it should be taught younger. I think people should stress in sex education, like, what can happen to you more. Because people have sex without thinking, and I think if they were a little bit more scared of the consequences, then I don't think it'd happen as much. And, there are a lot of sexually active teens my age."   —Maxon, 16, Missouri

"Sex ed. was not helpful"

"I took sex ed. in eighth grade, and it wasn't helpful at all. The teacher avoided talking about all the 'inappropriate' stuff. Sex ed. was not helpful because at that age, all the students did not know about any sexual activities or anything like that."

—Nicholas, 14, Illinois

Other teens say sex ed. isn't helpful because they feel like the teacher doesn't know what he or she is talking about. And if the students find the teacher less-than-credible, the student may tune out. To complicate matters even more, a teacher one student finds credible could be a teacher another student finds domineering or flaky—so you can't just rely on rumors about which teachers are supposedly great.

"I hated my health teacher"

"Last time I took health was my sophomore year of high school. I hated the class because the teacher was an extreme right wing Republican. We only covered sexual education for two weeks, and all that was taught to us was to say no to sex and to abstain. I was taught more in my eighth-grade health class in which we were even shown a video of how to put on a condom. I think sex ed. courses should teach kids that the best way to protect yourself from pregnancy or STDs is to abstain but that if you feel ready to have sex with the person you love and care about, you should prepare yourself for that sort of thing. Teach us about condoms and STDs and birth control, because the truth of the matter is that teenagers are going to have sex no matter what. The numbers may increase or decrease, but it is still going to happen so we should be informed of ways to protect ourselves if that is the choice we make."

—Laurie, 18, Illinois

"I knew more than my teachers"

"I have had sex ed. in fifth, sixth, seventh, and ninth grades. They didn't teach us much in elementary and middle school. I found the high school one to be more thorough. Although I did find that the teachers were lacking in knowledge, especially of birth control. I knew more than them! In the younger years, kids were very uncomfortable. They pretended they didn't want to hear about that stuff, but you could tell they wanted to listen and learn about what's going on with their bodies.

"My teachers at school, especially my ninth-grade year, were unknowledgeable about sex to the extent that they didn't tell them what to teach. They had a lesson plan, and they knew everything that had to do with that lesson plan, but when someone would ask a question, they would either not know the answer at all or make an educated guess. I knew a lot more about birth control and things to do with women, mostly because I see an OB-GYN, and I have done a lot of research. I was the one answering a lot of questions that people had."

—Suzanne, 15, Maryland

Still, for all the complaining about sex ed. most teens will admit that they learned something valuable from the class and were glad they took it. And teens who felt like they had a particularly good teacher or a good curriculum seem to know they are lucky and feel grateful for the opportunity to learn about these important topics.

"Sex ed. was really helpful"

"I had sex ed. in seventh grade, and it was actually really helpful. Our teacher was young, I think she was 25 years old, so it made the class a little more comfortable and not as weird if we had an old teacher.

"But people didn't really ask questions because it's kind of embarrassing to ask things in front of your friends. There was a day when people could put questions in a box anonymously and she would answer them, but I missed that day of class, so it didn't really help me. We learned about how babies are made and all that stuff.

"I already knew everything that we learned, but it still was helpful. We didn't really watch videos or stuff like that. Mostly we just talked."   —Caden, 13, Nebraska

Likewise, students who say their school doesn't offer sex ed. tend to feel like they are missing out on information that would be useful.

"There's a lot of kids here who could use sex ed."

"I was raised in a family that doesn't discuss sex that often. If we're ever talking about it, we're usually just joking around. To make matters more difficult, our school doesn't have a sex ed. class to teach kids about safe sex and how things work when you do have sex for the first time.

"Not having sex education in school bothers me because there's a lot of kids here who could use that class. The most we ever got was a nurse coming to talk to us about STDs. There are a few girls I know who do have STDs who could have been smarter about getting tested and stuff. There have been incidents with some of my friends who have had unprotected sex and thought they were pregnant, and they got tested and found out they weren't.

"I read a lot of books and stuff and magazines, and I've seen commercials where you can get info from the Internet on safe sex and stuff, so I research my information. Since I'm not learning it in school, I have to find out some way. I don't think most people are like me; I bet they go into most situations without knowing what to do."
—Bella, 15, South Dakota

REAL-WORLD ADVICE

Although some teens say sex ed. isn't helpful, it can and should be an excellent opportunity to get much-needed information to teens while they are somewhat of a captive audience. No matter what kind of class is being taught (or what kind of student you're dealing with), there are ways to help make sex ed. an experience that contributes to teens' knowledge base and helps them act intelligently and responsibly.

FIND OUT WHO'S TEACHING THE SEX ED. CLASS—
AND WHAT THEY'RE TEACHING

In many school districts, teaching sex education falls to a high school coach or health teacher who may not feel or be qualified for the job. Susie Wilson, founder of Sex, Etc., told me a story about a teen who told her he didn't think his sex ed. program was very effective because it was taught by his athletic coach—someone he had to see every day at team practice. The teenager felt uncomfortable asking this person questions or admitting there were things he didn't know because he was embarrassed; he likened the coach to being "sort of like my parents."

There is a sense among many teens that some of their teachers aren't well prepared to teach sex ed. Some teens went so far as to say that they could tell the teachers were uncomfortable with the material, and told me stories about teachers who only showed movies in the class and wouldn't accept any questions from the students. On the other hand, many schools do in fact present teens with teachers who are well versed in sex and sexuality education. There are some good training programs for teachers, and sometimes medical health professionals are even brought into schools to teach this class.

What's taught in sex ed. class is, to a degree, mandated by the state. I spoke with one educator who taught at an inner-city school where it was that school's policy to distribute condoms in health class. Other public-school educators talk about condoms only in terms of failure rates and lead discussions on marriage and how to find and keep a lifelong mate. As in every other subject, each sex ed. teacher brings his or her bias to the course. The teachers are following their school's guidelines, but how they choose to communicate the information can also have an effect on what students learn. There have also been reports of sex ed. classes and even textbooks that institutionalize misinformation by stating it as fact, including information about how effective various forms of birth control are or how STDs are transmitted.

With this wide a range of what's taught and who's teaching sex ed., it's worth it to get involved and find out who is teaching the sex education class and what information is being presented and emphasized. Look at the textbooks being used and at the homework materials, and talk about it as well. If anything sounds suspect, call the school for more information. You may be perfectly satisfied with the choices your school is making, and if you're not, you'll have the opportunity to make positive changes in your community.

I listened when my parents said:

"They told me about their teenage pregnancy, and that was enough."   —Girl, 15, California

BE THE SQUEAKY WHEEL

Every school district has a "health-curriculum committee." (This title varies from school to school, but the principal's office will know what you mean.) Any parent can call the principal's office and volunteer to be on this committee, which usually has several parent volunteers on board. If meetings conflict with work, there are other ways to be involved and review the minutes from the meetings. (The principal will have ideas.)

Talk the Talk: Teenagers Will Listen if You Say...

"So what are they teaching you in sex ed. these days? Tell me about something you found surprising." Or "Tell me about something you thought was true, but found out in class that you were wrong."

One parent of a fifth grader did this and learned that, "the teacher, who was a person in charge of sports and also health for our school system, had explained to my son that sexual intercourse was not pleasurable for women."

"You know, if you ever have a question that's not answered in sex ed., you can ask me and I'll find out the answer, or you can check out [websites you have screened here] for accurate information. I want you to have the information you need to make smart choices, when the time comes for you to make those choices, which I hope won't be until [your goal for your teen here]. What kinds of information do you think your school should teach in sex ed. class? What is being taught in your class? How could your class be improved? What's good about your class as it is?"

"I think the majority of parents probably don't know what's going on in their children's sex ed. classes," says Lloyd Kolbe, Ph.D., professor at Indiana University and the founding director of CDC's Division of Adolescent and School Health. "Oftentimes it's a vocal minority that will determine what kinds of education the schools are providing. I've seen individual schools and school districts and even states that will respond to concerns expressed by what I perceive to be minorities of people."

There's more information about abstinence-only sex education at abstinenceclearinghouse.com, and more about comprehensive sex education at advocatesforyouth.org, but rather than focusing on these catchphrases, use these resources to get ideas about what kinds of lessons and topics concerning sexuality and health you feel your teenager needs to be taught in school, and let your voice be heard. At the least, talk to your teenager about what kind of sex education he thinks he is getting versus what he thinks he *should* be getting. There have been several cases of students lobbying school boards for different and better sex education classes.

ASK QUESTIONS AND FILL IN THE BLANKS
Even if you see your teen's sex ed. curriculum (even if you help write it), you cannot monitor every class period or be privy to everything the teacher says. That's why it's important to ask your teen what he or she is learning in this class. Be open-ended in your questioning so you don't get "It's fine" as an answer.

ENLIST YOUR TEEN'S DOCTOR
Sex ed. should not begin and end at school. No matter how fantastic your child's sex education class is, it's not responsible for you to rely on her sex ed. teacher to adequately teach her everything, especially the facts about STD and unwanted-pregnancy prevention. Consider that in the Tell the Truth! survey only 52 percent of 17-year-olds reported that they had been taught how to put on a condom correctly. As awkward as it is, it's crucial that teens who are planning on using

---

Talk the Talk: What to Say to Your Teen's Doctor

[to the doctor]: "I'm noticing that my daughter is starting to be interested in boys [or: may be thinking about having sex], and even though I'm hoping she'll wait until [your goal for your teen here] to have sex, I want her to know the potential risks, and what all of the birth control and STD-prevention options are and how to use them correctly. Can you please go over these with her, and are you comfortable being very specific?" (See Chapter 9 for more about taking your teen to the doctor and how to talk to your teen about it before the visit.)

---

condoms for protection against pregnancy and (some) STDs fully understand how to do so.

If you don't feel comfortable talking this explicitly (and many parents don't), or you don't have access to all the latest information about STD and unwanted-pregnancy prevention, you can enlist your child's doctor to help. It can be either an OB/GYN (for girls) or a pediatrician or GP (for girls or boys). Jan Chapin, R.N., M.P.H., director of women's health for the American College of Obstetricians and Gynecologists, suggests calling your teen's doctor first and explaining to her why you want your teen to have a doctor's appointment and what you hope to accomplish. This is no time to be shy—you need to be candid so your doctor can help you help your teenager as much as possible.

It's ideal to begin this doctor/teen relationship before your teen is sexually active, so the trust will be there when they want to confide in the doctor or get medical information later.

If you don't know where to start looking for a new doctor, any clinic (such as Planned Parenthood) can put you in touch with a sex educator who can give your teen facts he can trust.

Keep in mind that your doctor's conversation with your teen will be confidential, so your only chance to weigh in on what gets said is before the visit. If you get the feeling that your doctor isn't comfortable having this kind of thorough conversation with your teen, call another doctor or clinic, until you find a doctor, physician's assistant, or nurse practitioner who is.

THE LAST WORD

It's not your responsibility to personally educate your teenager on every facet of sexual health, but it *is* your job to be sure he is educated before he makes what my parents used to refer to as "The Big Mistake," i.e., the one that changes your life forever, for the worse. If a teen is going to use condoms—or any other form of birth control or STD prevention as part of a plan—it's imperative they have a clear understanding of how to do so, as well as the necessary funding and support in place. Teens who want to remain abstinent throughout high school need to be given the skills and confidence required to be successful with that plan. Being sexually responsible is not just about making smart decisions; it's about figuring out how to plan ahead and implement those decisions, even under difficult or surprising circumstances. Sex education classes can be an ally in this goal, but only if the teacher is considered a source students can trust, the class is taught in a way that resonates with teens, and what's taught in the class reflects the information you feel your child needs to know.

It's Important to Talk to All Teens About **Gay Teens**

"I knew I was gay when I met this girl in 8th grade, and I loved her."
—Berry, 13, Maryland

"I take a verbal beating from guys at school." —Lazlo, 13, New York

Most parents have a vision of what they would like their teens to experience when it comes to sex, love, and relationships. As parents, we can't help but imagine what it will be like for our children to fall in love, start a family one day in the future, and experience all the joy relationships and family have brought us. Because most parents fantasize about a "dream life" for their kids, it's especially difficult for parents when expectations and visions for a child's love relationships clash with reality. These clashes can take many forms, such as a daughter dating a guy who's far too old, or a son who's chosen a girlfriend who's been known to abuse drugs. In these instances, there is no question but that the parent has the best interest of the teen in mind when trying to undo the situation.

But other times, these clashes can represent wishes parents have for their teen's love interests that are more matters of desire than danger—and in these instances, parents need to assess what is truly in the best interest of their child. Lots of teens tell me about parents disapproving of their relationships with someone of a different race, socioeconomic class, even different high school. And even though there are certainly parents who find out their child is gay and have a positive, receptive response to this news, over the years I have received many letters from teens who identify as gay, lesbian, or bisexual and fear (or actively experience) their parents' disapproval.

Though teens still tell me that it is often difficult for parents to accept the news that their teen is gay, I can report that over the past 10 years, the stories I'm hearing from gay teens have evolved greatly. When I was editing the "Sex and Body" column at *Seventeen* magazine a decade ago, teens would write saying they were in the closet and if they came out they were afraid they'd get beaten up at school, ostracized by their friends, and, most painfully, kicked out of their homes. Periodically we'd include one of these letters in the column and would often advise teens to stay in the closet if they feared that the consequences for coming out would be that parents would beat them up, kick them out of the house, or stop supporting them in college. Wait, we'd advise, until you can take care of yourself, emotionally and financially, if there is any risk that that support will be withdrawn when your parents hear your news.

Since then, there have been enormous advocacy and awareness campaigns on the part of groups like PFLAG (Parents, Families, and Friends of Lesbians and Gays; pflag.org) and GLSEN (Gay Lesbian and Straight Education Network; glsen.org), among others, and the letters from gay and lesbian teens have shifted from 100 percent "No way could I tell anyone" to, I'd say, at least 30 percent who now say, "My mom is cool about me being gay and my friends are, too." Clearly there is still a ways to go, and it is in large part up to parents to ensure that gay and lesbian high school students are treated with respect. For this reason and others (see below), it is important to talk to *all* teens about sexual orientation.

THINGS ARE GETTING BETTER—BUT THERE'S STILL MORE WORK TO BE DONE

Today, versus 10 years ago, there's more conversation about and less stigma attached to gay teens. The Internet has opened up a whole new avenue for gay teens and given them the opportunity to read stories of other teens who are grappling with the same issues. "I think there's much more openness about gay and lesbian life choices," says Susie Wilson, founder of the teen sexuality education website Sex, Etc. "They're all very eager for stories on Sex, Etc. about coming out."

Needless to say, typing in "gay teen" on a search engine will get your teen more than just coming-out stories from other teens, so it's important to review the rules of Internet safety (in Chapter 5) and screen sites that teens visit to be sure the content (as well as the advertisements on the site) are appropriate.

There are also more popular gay characters on TV and celebrities who are openly gay, which generates more public discussion about sexual identity. It's not a direct cause-and-effect thing, but more the subtle and ever-shifting movement in our culture toward less secrecy and more openness around some issues of sexuality which has helped some teens feel more comfortable with their identity and may even make it easier for those teens to talk about being gay with their family and friends.

"I can talk about my sexuality freely"

"I knew I was gay when I was about 13, but before that I had always looked at girls, and never known why I had the feelings that I did. I knew I was gay when I met this girl, when I was in eighth grade, and I loved her from the start. My brother told my parents for me, they were surprised and asked a lot of questions that made me really uncomfortable, I cried for a few days. But overall they are understanding.

"All my friends know I am gay. I have a lot of homosexual friends as well. But the straight friends I do have are very understanding for the most part, and I can talk about my sexuality freely.

"I go to a large public school. Most of the time I get treated fine, but there isn't a day where I don't get asked a question about my sexuality. Most of the time I just tell them its not their business. There are a lot of bisexual and homosexual people in my school, so I get treated pretty well by them of course. Some of the teachers give me dirty looks when I walk down the hallway holding hands with a female friend, and some have made smug comments. At times I feel uncomfortable in classrooms because students are rarely corrected for using terms like 'that's so gay' or more hateful words toward gay people.

"I guess if there was something I wanted to tell teens about my experience with being homosexual, is that I always look on the bright side of things. One day my fair maiden will come, and then everything will have been worth it. Being gay doesn't seem as bad at it might have a few years ago."   —Berry, 16, Maryland

The Internet has also been a resource for both grassroots and national advocacy and educational organizations to expand. These organizations, dedicated to making life easier for gay and lesbian teens, are certainly having a major impact. Teens who are involved in Gay-Straight Alliance (GSA) groups at school are far more likely to view a friend being gay as less of a big deal.

"None of the homosexuals at my school are persecuted"

"I attend a religious school, but there are still many openly gay and lesbian individuals. My school even has a club: the Gay and Straight Alliance. Going even further, none of the homosexual individuals at my school are persecuted because of their sexual preference.

"Last summer, I attended a program where I met kids from across the country. I was very surprised to learn that quite a few of them never knew any gay or lesbian people. In fact, my friends told me that at their high school, if anyone was to come out of the closet, they would be heavily bothered. Even though other places throughout the United States are accepting of same sex relationships, I am proud that the teenagers in my high school are, and have always been, very tolerant. Even though I am heterosexual, I am happy that the people at my school are mature enough and accepting enough to let their peers choose life paths for themselves with no teasing or violent behavior."   —Eva, 16, Hawaii

Still, a fair amount of gay teens feel that high school is torture, which is not only unjust, it's intolerable. No teen should feel persecuted at school or unsafe in their community. And coming out is still not safe for many teens, even within their own households. Even if a teen does not get kicked out or have funding withdrawn for their schooling, the taunting at school and/or the unremitting parental disapproval can be just as damaging to a teen's psyche.

"People scream faggot at you"

"I just wanted to give you personal kudos on writing this book. I know it is very difficult to talk to my parents about sexuality, and if it weren't for my own values I would be out having sex right now. I was raised in a very backwoods conservative town, so not very many people are accepting about anything untraditional. People scream faggot at you as you walk through the halls at school or at the mall. My mom would make digs about gays after I came out to her. One time out of nowhere my mom is just like 'All homos are going to Hell.'

"And the dating scene isn't easy to see if you are gay either. For example, if a straight person asks someone of the opposite sex out and they are gay they usually just say, 'No thanks I'm not into that.' But if a gay person asked a straight person out they get irate and start yelling and cussing and sometimes even get violent. And one of the main dating places for gay people are gay bars, and teens can't go in there unless they manage to sneak in and even then it isn't a good environment for getting a date. Most people just gasp at the mere thought of homosexuality even if they are homosexual. Because so many people in conservative communities that are homosexual are afraid to come out of the closet because they are afraid of what would happen, even if you were to ask another gay person out and they liked you too they would turn you down and make fun of you because they are afraid."   —Hayden, 16, Florida

"I can hardly mention being bisexual without an argument"

"I am close to my parents except for matters concerning sexuality. I wish that my father realized that people are born with their sexual orientation, and I wish badly that my mother was much more accepting about it. I can hardly mention anything about me being bisexual without getting into an argument with her.

"I keep bringing these things up because I always hope that she'll say, 'Yes, I love you, being bisexual is Okay, I don't mind,' but she never does. She said that she would not come to my wedding if I were to marry a girl.

"I had my friends over to throw a surprise birthday party for our friend. Toward the end of the party, we were all hanging out in the dining room when I confessed I was bisexual. They all nodded, said they didn't mind, and one of my friends mentioned how her mother had a gay friend, and how it was always fun to check out guys with him. One friend, however, abruptly stopped hanging around with me. I heard from numerous people that she was uncomfortable around me because I was a 'lesbian.'

"My favorite celebrity once said that she thought everyone was beautiful, and I think that is a wonderful way to view bisexuality. So I am open to marrying anyone: man, woman, or anyone in between."

—Janelle, 15, Massachusetts

"I kind of take a verbal beating"

"Yes I came out to my parents. First, I told my friends, then I told my mom. My mom and I were watching TV and I asked her if she had any gay, lesbian, or bisexual friends. She said, 'Of course, honey. Why?' I go, 'I'm gay, Mom.' She accepts me but she was crying because she didn't want any of the gay bashings to happen to me. My mom blabbed it to my dad. He loves me, too. They put me in a gay and lesbian club for kids called PFLAG.

"I kind of take a verbal beating from guys in my school. Actually, I am pressing charges against a kid for sexual harassment. I just couldn't take it anymore. Just the other day he came up to me, slapped my butt, and said 'Hey sexy!' I reported him to the principal. I found out that unfortunately straight people have more rights than gay people, and I really dislike that. A lot. Seriously, we should all have equal rights . . . I mean if you stab us we're going to bleed. It's not like we're dirt."

—Lazlo, 13, New York

If gay and lesbian teens are being treated unfairly at school or in the community, you can change that. Even if your teen is not gay, intolerance is bad for all teens, and when it's permitted to thrive or is fostered by certain attitudes it breeds intolerance to other groups within that community—like a bad virus. Ritch Savin-Williams, Ph.D., author of *Mom, Dad, I'm Gay* and professor of developmental and clinical psychology at Cornell University, says you don't have to be a full-blown activist to make a difference in your community. "Just make sure that the institutions you're a part of—whether it be church, synagogue, school system—are fair and tolerant. You have every right to demand that of the school system, to say 'I want to make sure that my kid is safe and not being abused, or harassed by teachers, and if he is, you better be sure I'm going to make noise about it.' "

✳ How Many Gay Young People Are Victimized? ✳

About 50% of 681 gay youth (age 13 to 25) interviewed online by the Outproud/Oasis Internet Survey had endured some form of victimization (such as being insulted, threatened with physical violence, or beaten) based on sexual orientation.
—*Journal of Clinical Child and Adolescent Psychology,* 2003

Whether it's writing a letter to the principal or sending an e-mail to a teacher, any time a parent or concerned adult takes even the smallest of steps to battle intolerance, that person is not only setting an amazing example for teens, they're also making the teens' environment safer and better for all teens.

TALKING ABOUT BEING GAY
WON'T MAKE A TEEN GAY

Many parents express concern that by bringing up the topic of being gay, they will be introducing the idea to their teen or preteen, thereby running the risk of "making them gay."

That's simply not true, says Savin-Williams, who has conversed with thousands of teens while conducting research for studies and books over the course of 20 years. "I think that's just part of the sex phobia that's going around—it doesn't happen."

"I told my mother very directly"

"I didn't just wake up one morning and think 'Gosh. I'm gay. How dreadful' or see a boy and think, 'He's really hot. I guess that means I'm gay.'

"I told my mother very directly. I wanted to make sure that we were clear on that issue. I've told some other people, but only in response to questions that they might have posed to me. I would not dream of pushing my sexuality onto anyone. My friends' responses have been overwhelmingly positive. I see my sexuality as being a very private matter; there are aspects of one's life that are appropriate to be shared.

"I don't mind at all not being able to come out to everyone because I do care about others' reactions, and if they won't like it, why rub their faces in it? It's courteous to steer away from subjects that are controversial.

"And as for talking to ones' parents, I would steer away from drama, and not have a huge amount of buildup. That's probably unnecessary."   —Oren, 14, Connecticut

I listened when my parents said:

"You can always be open with me."   —Girl 17, California

Parents Speak Out:
"My teen was afraid to tell me"

"When my son came out to me, he was very afraid, and crying, and he said, 'You're not going to like this.' I wasn't surprised that he was gay. In preschool, every single day he'd go in and put on the pink fairy dress. I said: 'As long as you're right with God it's okay with me.' What I mean by that is, as long as you know in your heart that you're doing what God wants you to do. I felt sad because I'm afraid for him.

"You know, because you're a parent: you would sooner die yourself 10 times over than have anything happen to your child. At his last school, he was beat up in the bathroom. This isn't like being teased for your funny last name or your ears. This is a different kind of violence. This is getting beaten bloody and left for dead. My biggest concern is, he's not very masculine the way society thinks of being masculine. He's pretty much the stereotype, and he has been and will be a target.

"Listen, I don't think anybody looks at their kid when they're born and says 'Oh God, I hope you grow up to be gay.' I don't think it's a disability, not at all. But it's a harder life."

—Nevada mother of a teenage son

While talking about being gay won't make a teen gay, *not* talking about it means the teen is left guessing how his parents feel about the issue (and, quite possibly, guessing incorrectly). This is another opportunity for parents to connect and make it clear that their love is unconditional, and/or to simply show teens by example how extremely important it is that everyone in the family judge others based on their character and not based on who they are attracted to.

TIP: Check out comingoutstories.com to read stories from teens (15 and older) and how they came out. These stories offer a lot of insight and perspective into what it's like for them. YoungGayAmerica.com also has resources as well as stories from teens.

REAL-WORLD ADVICE

Remember how teens often misunderstand what parents are trying to tell them? This also holds true for talking about sexual identity. "Sometimes parents think that saying 'Hey I have gay friends' or watching *Will and Grace* will deliver a message," says Savin-

Williams. "Or if they say to the kids, 'Hey, if there's anything you ever want to talk about, just let me know,' they think that will be an opening." But these messages are too subtle and too easy for teens to miss. To make it clear that it's okay to talk openly about homosexuality, parents need to explicitly send the message that respect and tolerance are highly valued and expected. The following talking tips will help make that point.

SAY POSITIVE THINGS ABOUT GAY PEOPLE

By the time a child is 8 or 9, she probably knows that some people are gay. She's probably also heard lots of negative slurs against gay people. To counterbalance that, you can give her truths as you know them about gay people, especially if you have friends or relatives who are gay that you can talk about specifically.

TIP: If you suspect your teen wants to talk about same-sex attraction, consider having her talk to a gay relative or friend whom you admire and trust.

Also be cautious that you're not making assumptions about a child from a young age that could make it hard for him to talk to you later. For instance, if you're always talking about how other little girls are "flirting" with him, that's sending the subtle message that you expect your child to be attracted to the opposite gender.

✳ Exclusive National Survey Results ✳
Teens: Tell the Truth!

Who would you talk to first about "being gay"?

Boys: 37% parents   11% a friend

Girls: 35% parents   21% a friend

Talk the Talk: Teenagers Will Listen if You Say...

"I think it's great how in-love Sarah and Rebecca seem, and what caring parents they are. Ashley is lucky to have moms that love her so much."

"It must have been hard for Travis to tell his dad that he's gay. That was brave of him."

AVOID LABELS

Part the challenge of being a teen is figuring out what you want in life and who you are. Many people now ascribe to the theory that sexuality is more of a spectrum than a hard-and-fast identity, especially during the teen years, which are all about exploration and experimentation. It can be very confusing, and overwhelming, for a teen to feel like she needs to label herself a lesbian because she is experiencing a same-sex attraction this week or toward just one girl. She may, in fact, identify as a lesbian when she's older, but for now it makes sense for her language—and yours—to label just her feelings, not her as a person. This kind of open speaking can really help a teenager figure out who she is in a calm, reality-based environment rather than a fearful, judging, chaotic one.

Teens whose parents take this approach feel supported. "My mother knew right from the start, when I told her that I wasn't sure if I was straight," says Marcia, 13, from California. "She said that it was all right, that she'd accept me any way I was. She also said that I shouldn't say that I was something when I hadn't had time to experiment with different kinds of relationships. It's taken her a little time to, but I think she's gotten used to it, and she's been really supportive of me through this difficult time in my life."

If your teen starts to express (or you suspect) that he or she is ex-

Talk the Talk: Teenagers Will Listen if You Say...

"You can always talk to me about relationships or who you're attracted to or really anything that's on your mind. And if you don't feel like you can talk with me about something, please talk with [adult you trust with your teen's confidences here]."

"I want you to know that I love you unconditionally, no matter who you fall in love with or who you're attracted to. I will always love you and hope you can always feel comfortable talking to me about this kind of thing."

"I think it's important for you to leave all options open, and I just want you to know that. I know you're going to eventually follow your heart and feel comfortable with someone you're in love with, and I want that for you—I want for you to be in love with someone special. But for now, don't close any doors, because the way you feel now may not reflect the way you'll feel in 10 years. It may—but it also may not, so I want you to always have choices."

periencing same-sex attraction, without being dismissive of those feelings, encourage your teen to keep his or her options open, because sometimes feelings teens have at 13 or 14 do not translate to how they feel sexually at 18 or 19. Then again, sometimes they do. This is not an excuse for you to make your teen feel "I hope you won't be gay when you get older," because that can be very damaging to the teen's self-esteem if indeed he or she does identify as gay later in life.

TIP: Learning that a teen is gay may mean grieving for the life you had hoped he or she would lead. Allow time for this process, and don't respond immediately if you're afraid you can't be support or will seem hostile.

STARTING THIS CONVERSATION

What if you think your teen is gay and she isn't telling you? Give it some time and drop the lines in "Avoid Labels" and "Say positive Things About Gay People" (earlier in this chapter). She may open up. Remember that this is a huge deal to your teen and she may fear your rejection, so don't expect her to rush to tell you even if you have an otherwise open relationship.

No matter what, "it's not without consequences, coming out to your parents," says Rosemary Prentice, a family nurse practitioner who is on the faculty at the University of Maine. And waiting awhile doesn't hurt, especially if you feel in your heart that your teen is really not ready to talk about this issue yet. It's not fair to pump him for information just to satisfy your curiosity. If, however, you suspect that your teen is gay and may be getting into a relationship without all the information he needs to be safe, then you need to bring it up.

TIP: Parents of gay teens also need to talk to them about pregnancy and STD prevention (see Chapter 9).

WHAT NOT TO SAY

Without meaning to, sometimes parents who are feeling uncomfortable can say things that will slam shut the proverbial doors of communication. "You're not gay, are you?" is one that Jeanne Stanley says many of her gay teen clients have noted was their parents' way of bringing up the topic. Another she's heard, when a teen brings up the idea of same-sex attraction, is "Don't be ridiculous."

Talk the Talk: Teenagers Will Listen if You Say...

"It feels like maybe there's something you may not be sharing with me, and I want you to understand that I love you unconditionally and no matter what you're feeling, I totally accept you. You don't have to share anything with me that you don't want to, but if you do decide to confide in me, I promise to listen to you with an open mind and an open heart. Is there anything you want to say to me?"

"It seems like you are having some really intense relationships with other guys. Do you agree with this? How are you feeling about it? Do you think this might be important for your future?"

Many gay teens have told me that their parents reacted with great sadness, saying that they feared the teen would have an incredibly hard life fraught with teasing and worse, possible violence. Though there are still challenges to being gay, telling this to a teen won't change his identity. A more positive approach is to acknowledge that being attracted to someone of the same sex can be difficult and then tell your teen that you'll stand by her and be sure her school, community, and home are safe and respectful places for her to be.

THE LAST WORD

It's helpful to think about these conversations before your teenager or another teenager in your life that you care about catches you off-guard by asking you to talk about sexual orientation. Your initial reaction to the news will have a big impact on how he or she feels about sharing all sorts of important information with you, now and in the future.

Thinking About **Teen Love** as "Puppy Love" Is a Big Mistake

*** Exclusive National Survey Results ***
Teens: Tell the Truth!

15% of teens ages (12 to 17) feel the right time for someone to lose their virginity is "whenever they're in love."

*

"I love my girlfriend, but sex has nothing to do with love."

—Glen, 17, Texas

*

"The word love is very strong . . . Love to me means forever, for infinity—for eternity."

—Meryl, 15, California

Even with all the talk about "blowjob buses" and "friends with benefits," love is still very much on teens' minds and is a big part of their lives. So many teens, even those as young as 13, tell me that they feel very much in love. I always get scads of letters from girls in love, asking, in various ways, "Does he like me?" This question is usually embedded within long stories about what she said, then he said, then she said, then he said . . . "Does he like me?" And many a guy, though he may never admit it to his friends, has expressed to me a similar curiosity about not just how to get a girl to have sex with him but how to get her to like him.

The love these teens describe is not "puppy love," as many parents would dismiss teen infatuation, but real, heart-wrenching, bone-crushing love, both requited and unrequited. And if you visit any chat rooms that cater to teens who want to talk about dating, you'll notice that much of the chatter is about love.

Since teens usually *want* to talk about love, it's an easy opening to begin talking to them about the whole concept of relationships and sex. Other reasons it's so important to know what's going on with teens and love:

SEX TRIGGERS LOVE

It's true; I've heard from many teens who claim they "can't wait" to lose their virginity or say they are having sex with someone they "like but don't feel that close to." Yet many teens also report that after having sex they felt a rush of emotions they didn't understand.

"She thinks she's in love"

"My friend has always been picked on by boys, mostly because she's tall, so she's never had a boyfriend, never been kissed. She liked this kid for years, and a few nights ago she she gave him head because she thought it would lead to something more. The next day the guy was bragging about how he used her to get what he wanted. I told my friend, listen, you knew he was a player, what you did has consequences. And she looked at me and told me that she loved him."

—Petra, 15, Oklahoma

As discussed in Chapter 2, this story illustrates the point that boys and girls often have different expectations concerning what will happen after fooling around. This girl thought that by fooling around with a guy, she might be able to get him to love her the way she feels in love with him. Unfortunately, as Petra told me, the guy did not feel the same way. Sadly for girls in this situation, the love they felt for the guy intensifies after fooling around, while if the guy never felt love to begin with, his feelings for the girl rarely bloom into love as a result of fooling around.

"There was a day when a man who trifled with a woman's feelings would be ostracized from polite society," says Steven Rhoads, Ph.D., who is also the author of *Taking Sex Differences Seriously* and a professor of public policy at the University of Virginia. "We're a long way from that but need to let guys know that young women are likely to care more than the guy does before agreeing to any given sexual activity. At the very least, young men should surely be told that if, to get sex, he tells a girl he loves her when he does not, it is shameful behavior."

Although it's more common for girls to have hurt feelings after a "hookup gone bad," boys are by no means immune. "Sexual intimacy is going to trigger romantic intimacy and emotional intimacy," says psychologist Jeanne Stanley. Girls and guys tell me that they went into a situation thinking they were going to fool around, no strings attached, but ended up feeling regretful afterward.

TIP: Gently tell teens that many of the "sayings" about love (like "love conquers all," "all you need is love," and "all's fair in love") don't hold true for many circumstances. Give examples.

LOVE TRIGGERS SEX

Teens, especially girls, may not want to envision themselves as "planning to have sex," primarily because they feel like it's not romantic and kind of "slutty" to do so. This attitude, however, is in direct conflict with what we would like, which is for both partners to be emotionally and literally prepared for sex, including having protection against pregnancy and STDs, before said sex takes place. The hyper-romanticizing of sex has many consequences, which are talked about throughout this book, but one that applies here is that many girls have this fantasy that they need to be swept away, romanced off their feet, swooning-in-love, and then the sex will "just kind of happen."

"I trust him with everything"

"Parents don't understand what it's like to be a teen now. I mean sure it was basically the same but small details change the whole big picture. My school is a strange place. If you have sex you're a slut but if you don't have sex you'll never get a date until you do. If you're wondering, I am a virgin.

"I met this guy at a cookout. He's everything any girl could want in a guy. He keeps me laughing, he's someone I can talk to forever, not to mention he's a wicked cutie. We've become good friends and we've talked about a lot of things I don't even talk to my parents and close friends about. We talked about our secrets no one else knows. I'm usually shy around people I like, but around him I'm loud and I talk . . . I even told him that I like him to his face. I love being open with him, and I trust him enough with it all. I got to tell him about how I want to lose my virginity to a virgin so it's something special between me and him, and that I want to really be in love with the person first.

"A teenage girl's heart is a deep hole of secrets and lies, giggles and tears. It's something that no one can really understand."

—Zoe, 13, Massachusetts

Elizabeth Casparian, Ph.D., who answered teen's questions by the thousand for the website Sex, Etc. for five years and is now the director of educational programs at HiTOPs, a teen-health education center based in New Jersey, says she hears less than she would like to about love. "But when we do hear about it, it really is the question 'How do I know if I'm really in love?' " Unfortunately, Casparian says, she worries that teens are asking how to tell if they're in love because if they are, then they feel it's "okay" to have sex—or "okay" to have sex without using condoms. "Some teens want to know what love is so they can say, 'Well I'm in love and love conquers all. I don't have to be responsible, I was swept away! I'm in love!' " So instead of feeling like love means they don't have to prove anything by having sex, love serves as a justification for fooling around or having sex.

"I really liked him . . . and I thought he liked me"

"I thought it was great when you decided to write this book. I don't talk about my personal life with anyone, because in a little town like this, everyone will know by the end of the school day. . . .

"When I was a freshman in high school, I really liked this guy. He was my dream of a perfect guy . . . Whenever he was around, I couldn't help but stare. He was so gorgeous, and all the girls liked him. This guy said that he liked me . . . and he said that I was pretty. I am a person with 'okay' self-esteem. I think I am pretty, but to hear it from a guy that I like . . . It was amazing. This boy continued to tell me he liked me, and tell me I was pretty . . . This got to the extent where I actually thought that he liked me. Deep down, I thought he liked me. What else would a 16-year-old girl do?

"I made out with him and he felt me up, and he wanted to do more. But I knew it wasn't right, so I told him no. I really liked this guy, but I had this little voice in my head saying 'Don't do it.' "

—Daria, 16, Iowa

This teen had the strength to stop fooling around when she stopped feeling comfortable with what was going on (which was a good thing, because as she had feared, the guy she was fooling around with did in fact tell the whole school about it the next day). But feeling in love can make it that much more difficult for some teens to know where to draw the line.

LOVE OR LUST: THAT IS THE QUESTION

I've certainly heard from teen guys who are romantic and want to find love or feel they are very much in love. At the same time, a good deal of girls report to me that high school guys are primarily interested in sex while girls are interested in love. There is also a feeling, among both guys and girls, that many girls view sex as a way to get and keep a guy's love. Of course, girls have hormones too, and this is not to take anything away from any of those feelings and desires girls have. All this points to an issue that even adults struggle with: what's the difference between love and lust? For teens, it's very much a blurry line.

Haley, 14, from California, explains: "I have just entered high school, and already drama has hit. I'm an observer; I always ask what's going on in people's lives. The chances of a girl finding a nice guy that cares more about love than sex is 2 out of 3,000. I have a lot of guy friends, and they tell me that all they care about is sex. And the guys know girls will do anything just to keep their man. If you really want to know about relationships all you need to know is this: girls will do anything to get a guy, and guys know this. Girls think they're in love when really the guy just wants them for sex. Girls think if they're giving a guy blowjobs, their man will stay around. All of my friends are looking for love, and all these guys are doing is taking advantage of them."

Naturally, this doesn't apply to all guys. In the Tell the Truth! survey, 70 percent of guys and 85 percent of girls agreed: "Sex should be romantic." This points to a feeling among the vast majority of guys that there should be love and romance in a sexual relationship. A question is, though, do guys and girls think of love the same way? From what teens tell me, high school girls feel love as more of a deep, emotional, soul-searching connection, whereas guys tend to express a less complicated version, a very intense "like."

"Sex has nothing to do with love"

"Most kids are having sex. People have been doing it for a while. It's life. It's so old, I don't even want to do it no more. It's so easy to do. I can go to the mall, get a girl, take her to my house, and do it. That's no fun, that's not good. I want a challenge to get her number. It's gonna take seeing her three or four dates to kiss her. I don't want to talk to her for 35 minutes and get in her pants. How many people has she done that with, and what kind of disease she got?

"I have a girlfriend. I just stick to me and my girl. Hell no we don't sleep with other people. I'll be mad; I would kill that person. Because I love my girl. We've known each other forever. I messed up once, and I told her. And when I messed up, when I did it, I didn't know what I had 'til I did it. I love her, my girlfriend, but sex has nothing to do with love. Our hormones are going crazy. When I hit the age of 14, my hormones were off the wall. I couldn't control it. It aggravates you.

"My mom knows I do it, have sex. She doesn't try to stop me, cause if kids want to have sex they're going to have sex whether parents like it or not.

"When I was 11, my mom's like, 'You don't need to be having sex, God doesn't like that, you should wait 'til you get married. God says you should wait 'til you get married.' But she knows I'm not going to. She does it! She tells you not to have sex, but still, they were doing it when they were our age, too."   —Glen, 17, Texas

---

TIP: Be sure boys know that if they "kiss and tell," their girlfriend can get a bad reputation, which can be very damaging to her self-esteem.

"The word love is very strong"

"I'm a major hopeless romantic, but I personally have a strong belief that you can't necessarily be in love at this age. I think it's way sweet hearing the stories of people who where high school sweethearts. It does happen to those very few, but I don't believe that when young people say they are in love it is for real. The word *love* is very strong.

"The relationships we have now are going to shape how we decide who we want to spend the rest of our life with in the future. I've had personal experiences where I thought maybe it was love but it wasn't because a couple weeks later I was bored with him and didn't necessarily want to be around him anymore. Love to me means forever, for infinity—for eternity. It's too much of a strong word to be saying to every person you have a feeling for. I think young people should not necessarily take relationships so seriously. I've seen too many people get their hearts broken and it messes them up. They do eventually get over it, but for that month that they have heartbreak everything drops, how they do in school, in sports, everything. I think young people including myself should stop and just really think about what love is before we go around saying it."   —Meryl, 15, California

For most teens, feelings of love and sex are very much intertwined, so it's important to acknowledge love when you're talking about sex and desire, because love has a great impact on teens' decisions in this area.

TIP: Realize that your teen feels like she knows more about love than you do. Your conversations will have the most impact if you do not dismiss this as a possibility.

REAL-WORLD ADVICE

The most important thing when talking to teens about love is to remember how potent and powerful an emotion love is. People kill and start wars over love. People move cross-country, change jobs, and make enormous sacrifices for love. Perhaps you're thinking, *Sure, adults do those things. But we're talking about teenagers here.* Ah, yes—that brings me to my first point.

DON'T DISMISS TEEN LOVE

If anything, teenagers feel their emotions *more* passionately than adults do. So it's often immensely frustrating for them to be told that it's "just their hormones" or "just their emotions running wild." Imagine someone telling you that you may think you're in love, but you're not really in love, because you don't know what love truly is. How infuriating! Even if you honestly believe this to be true, this is one of those "conversation stoppers" that will not only cause your teen to shut down and stop communicating with you on this topic, it'll also contribute to her general feeling that you really don't understand her or anything that's going on in her life.

That said, it can be hard to listen to your 13-year-old insist he's found the love of his life and plans to be with her forevermore. So this is where you start asking questions. Not drill-sergeant questions that make him feel attacked; rather, "I'm interested" questions that make him feel supported and like you truly care about what's going on with him.

The trick here is not merely to go on an information quest, but rather to get your teenager talking to you about his feelings and be-

---

Talk the Talk: Teenagers Will Listen if You Say...

"Tell me more about her—what do you like about her so much?"

"What kinds of things do you like to do together?"

"Do the two of you have lots of friends in common?"

havior regarding his new love interest. What if he backs down and doesn't want to say anything or offers one-word responses? That's fine. You don't have to keep hammering him with questions. Just leave it with, "Well this is very interesting and I'm happy you've found someone who makes you so happy. I hope we can talk more about her soon."

What if you're convinced that this person is wrong, wrong, wrong for your teen? This is the hard part: you have to keep that to yourself. Teens are at the stage of their lives when they are learning who they are and how to interface with the world around them, and they are going to make some mistakes. Falling in love with someone who doesn't love him back or going on a date with a guy who isn't smart enough for her are mistakes your teen can learn from. The caveat is that if they're in love with someone clearly inappropriate (someone far older, or a person you know for a fact is into drugs or alcohol, a convicted felon), in which case you need to calmly but firmly tell your teen you won't allow the relationship, and use any means necessary to enforce your authority here. But use this power wisely, because if you're overreacting and your teen goes behind your back and nothing bad happens, you will have lost a lot of credibility.

As Haley, 14, from California puts it, it's hard to confide in your parents when you feel like they're always yelling at you, preaching, or overreacting: "Talking to your parents about what goes on in your school life is hard. It's hard to talk to your mom about boys because she acts like we're the best of friends, and then the next day she yells at me for not having the room clean. Many of my friends keep their relationships a secret, or they just lie to their parents. It's just hard to talk to them about relationships because they always seem to want to give you lessons, like don't have sex, and be careful, don't do drugs or don't let this guy take advantage of you. It's like they're only reading out of a book and not really listening to what you say."

To prove that you are listening, ask follow-up questions the next day, or week, to see how things have turned out. Refrain from teasing, which can be very hurtful and make a teenager shut down. Also try not to judge, which includes not saying, "It seems like you have a new love interest every five minutes." Of course she does.

TIP: Don't be 100 percent cynical about love, even if Cupid has been unkind to you. You'll make your teen feel like he can't share anything about love with you.

TALK ABOUT WHAT LOVE IS—AND ISN'T

Since teens are "trying on" the idea of love, they can easily get sucked into unhealthy relationship patterns. Even though you want to let your teen make some mistakes, you want to help her avoid being in a relationship (or getting stuck in one) where she's getting verbally or emotionally abused, or he's having every facet of his life controlled by a 14-year-old girl. Teens who witness healthy relationships are less susceptible to this, and conversely, teens who witness unhealthy relationships are more likely (though not destined) to emulate them. So talk openly about what love is and how people who love each other act. It might be helpful to draw up a list of loving versus nonloving behaviors. You could ask your teenager to do the same and compare notes. Some examples that might be on your list:

People who love each other:

- **Think about and respect each other's feelings, know that each is a separate person with their own friends and activities**

- **Encourage each other to have other friends and do their own activities**

- **Never hit each other or call each other names**

- **Sometimes fight, but don't fight the majority of the time they're together**

- **Don't tease each other in a way that is mean or hurtful**

- **Don't pressure each other to do things they don't want to do (especially sexually)**

... and so on.

If you're concerned that your teen is in an unhealthy or abusive relationship, it's important to get them help right away. Some signs to be aware of: your teen's boyfriend or girlfriend seems very jealous, makes constant demands that your teen feels a need to comply with (including demands about what they wear or where they go), is constantly "checking up on" your teen, or just seems to be making your teen more stressed out and unhappy than happy. It can be hard to notice dating abuse because of the abused teenager's tendency to make excuses for the abusing partner, so err on the side of caution—and trust your instincts. Dating abuse is serious; emotional abuse can make teens feel suicidal and depressed and can escalate to physical abuse. Check out the National Youth Violence Prevention Resource Center at safeyouth.org or call 1-866-SAFEYOUTH for resources and more information.

Your teen should come up with some thoughts, but you can steer the conversation so you touch upon the ideas that it's not okay for a boyfriend/girlfriend to make you feel bad, call you names ("Is it okay to call each other names?"), disrespect you, or cheat on you. Remember that for your teenager, the social currency of having a boyfriend is difficult to overcome, so don't dismiss that when you're trying to talk to her about whether this relationship is good for her. If you believe she's being abused or even that the relationship is headed in that direction, don't merely forbid her to see him—get help for her so she can see for herself why she doesn't want to be with him.

TIP: When watching movies or TV shows, rate the quality of the relationships people are having and explain why you feel that way. Ask your teen, "What would you do if you were in the same situation as the character on this show?"

> ### *Talk the Talk: Teenagers Will Listen if You Say...*
>
> "I've noticed that your new guy often asks you where you're going and when you'll be home. Do you ever feel like he's checking up on you too much? Because when you love someone, you have to trust them too. Do you feel like he trusts you? Let's talk about what you think is acceptable and what's not acceptable behavior in a boyfriend [girlfriend] in general. Obviously, it's never acceptable for anyone to hit you or even make you think they're going to hit you. What else is unacceptable? Of course it's not enough for a boyfriend to just be 'acceptable,' right? What behaviors do you expect from a boyfriend? How should he make you feel? What should he do to make you feel that way?"

DON'T PRESSURE TEENS TO BE IN LOVE

From the time a parent takes a child to the playground and people say "Oh, Timmy, Susie's flirting with you!" most teens have received constant, sometimes subtle—sometimes not—messages that having a boyfriend/girlfriend is better than not. Sometimes in an effort to relate to teens it can be easy to subtly pass on the message that you'd be impressed or particularly interested in them if they had a relationship with the opposite sex. This seems particularly true of guys and their dads; some guys have told me that they felt like if they didn't get a relationship going with a girl soon their dad might think they were gay. As one New York father of two girls put it, "When we were kids, it was pretty tough to have sex in ninth grade, tenth grade, and I think for many fathers . . . it's like having your son be a football player when you weren't."

If you have a boy, you may have noticed that whenever you're at a family gathering the guys in the room all ask him if he has a girlfriend, with that sly nod-and-wink. Women may be asking your daughter if she's "in love" yet. These questions, while meant to be in

Talk the Talk: Teenagers Will Listen if You Say...

"Are you still having fun dating Susan? Sometimes after you hang up the phone with her you seem really sad. If dating her starts to be less fun, you could consider breaking up with her—because it should be mostly fun to be in love. Let me know if you want to talk about this more."

"I know it seems like everyone has a boyfriend, but really, what percentage of kids in your grade are part of a couple? What could you be doing that would help you to meet more people and different kinds of people?"

This is a great opportunity to help your teenager think about clubs, jobs, volunteering, activism—whatever they're interested in.

good fun or just curiosity or genuine interest, put subtle pressure on teens to fall in love and to be in a relationship, sometimes before they're really ready to even start thinking about it.

Teens pressure each other as well. Many teens tell me that it's much cooler to be in a relationship than to be single, even as young as eighth grade. Empower your teenager to feel good about himself, whether he's in a relationship or not, by encouraging him to participate in programs that will make him feel a part of something worthwhile. And help her see that breaking up with someone who is no longer fun to date is far better than dating someone she's not into anymore. Sometimes, like a cat up a tree, a teenager can get into a relationship and not know how to get out.

RESPECT THE POWER OF DESIRE

Back to the talk of "hormones run amok"—don't take this situation lightly. Teenage guys and girls have sex on the brain, in part, because they are biologically programmed to. For girls, experiencing these intense feelings of desire can sometimes translate in their brains as "I'm in love." Especially if they believe, as many do, that it's wrong to have sex without love, this can be a way for her to justify to herself why she feels like having sex (without feeling like "then I must be a slut"). And this sequence can happen to guys as well, which is why it's important not to be dismissive of the fact that desire is a very real feeling and one that can at times be all-encompassing. It is natural for teens to feel desire, and they shouldn't be made to feel bad or guilty about it. You can normalize desire by talking and allowing your teens to talk about it. And allow your teenager to talk about love, without making her feel that her feelings are not valid due to her age. The more you can listen to her talking about love, the closer (and more connected) she will feel to you.

The key here is to separate for your teen the feelings of being in love with those of desire, and to communicate that they do not have to be in love to be attracted to someone, and being in love with someone does not mean that they necessarily have to or will fool around with them.

DON'T LET YOUR TEEN DATE BEHIND YOUR BACK

The last thing you want is for your teenager to be dating someone and hiding it from you. As with sneaking sex, sneaking a whole relationship is a recipe for disaster (including increased risk of unwanted pregnancy or STDs). But if a teen fears you'll disapprove or is generally afraid to tell you things, she'll be tempted to date behind your back and be all the less likely to come to you if and when she really needs your guidance, advice, support, and help.

"A lot of times we create a pact with our kids" says Laura Gauld, director of family education at the Hyde Schools and coauthor of *The Biggest Job We'll Ever Have*. "They don't want to tell us the truth,

Talk the Talk: Teenagers Will Listen if You Say...

"This may be a weird question, but do you know the difference between love and lust? It's easy to get them confused. I think love is when you know someone for a long time and feel close to them because you have mutual like and respect and things in common and just want to be together. Lust is more of a physical thing, when you're drawn to someone and sometimes you can feel like you *need* to fool around with them. Just because you feel desire for someone doesn't mean you're in love with them, and it doesn't mean you have to fool around with them, either." To get them thinking about and separating the two, the next time you're watching TV and a couple starts making out, you can ask your teen: love or lust?

"Ever notice how in movies the couple gets swept away and ends up having sex because they're so driven by their hormones and feelings of love? Can you think of an example of what I'm talking about?" [Have some examples ready in case your teen can't think of any.] "That makes for a good story, but it doesn't usually happen that way in life, because being in love means more than sex; it means taking care of each other. Couples who care about each other talk about sex before they do it and plan to use birth control and protection against STDs. I hope that when you have sex, which I hope won't be until [your goal here], you'll have lots of conversations about it before you do it. Because being 'swept away' without consequences only happens in the movies. What kinds of things do you think you need to talk about with a partner before you have sex?" Help steer him toward birth control, STD prevention, and also *feelings*—like how they'll both feel afterward and whether this signifies a new level of commitment."

and we don't want to know the truth." And with good reason: things will sometimes get ugly when you press for the truth. You may find out that your daughter is in love with the son of parents that you hate. Or that your son is in love with someone three years younger and you don't think that's right. No matter what the truth turns out to be, it's better to have the argument than not get the opportunity to offer your guidance and information.

The truth will feel less scary if you've told your teenager what you expect from him in terms of a love relationship. Many teens tell me with a hint of pride that they were not allowed to date until a certain age or grade. I get the feeling it takes the pressure off them and makes them feel very protected by their parents. Other teens speak with fear about being exposed as having a boyfriend who was from another part of town or was a different race or religion. I often wonder if these teens' parents would really be so judgmental about who they were dating or if that's simply the teens' perception, perhaps based on a stray remark rather than the parents' actual feelings about the matter.

THE LAST WORD

Love can be incredibly powerful. Remember when you first got married or fell in love and had that "it's us against the world" feeling, where nothing could come between you and your partner? Teens have that feeling, too, that exciting feeling of having found someone to share secrets and hopes and new experiences with. Your challenge is to allow your teen to experience these feelings, even let him enjoy them, without making him feel like it's "them against you." You don't want to be on the other side of their pact, so they feel like it's really in everyone's best interest if they hide information from you. Because once teens start keeping secrets, it can be very hard for them to know what to share.

Talk the Talk: Teenagers Will Listen if You Say...

"What kinds of things do you think people lie to their parents about? It's important to me that you always tell me the truth, even if you think it will make me feel angry or disappointed. I'm not going to say it'll always be easy, but it's not my job as your parent to always have it easy. I need to know what's going on in your life so I can be here for you. Will you promise me not to lie? You don't have to tell me every detail! But please don't lie to me, especially about the big stuff like alcohol or drugs or sex—or love."

"If you ever get in trouble or need my help, even if it's something very serious like getting someone pregnant or catching an STD, I'm not going to say it'll be easy, but I want you to come to me so I can help you. I realize that you're going to make mistakes and make decisions that I might not have chosen for you. No matter what, I love you and will always want to do whatever I can to help you."

Always remember that your teen's biggest, darkest fear is losing love: Yours. By keeping lines of communication open, you're helping your teen see that it is possible to tell you anything without risking losing your love.

Too Many Teens Still Don't Know How to Avoid STDs and Unwanted Pregnancy

* **Exclusive National Survey Results** *
Teens: Tell the Truth!

How concerned would you be about
getting pregnant/getting someone pregnant?

56% Extremely concerned; I'd feel like my life was basically over.

28% Very concerned; I wouldn't be able to think about anything else.

6% Concerned, but I'd recover.

2% A little concerned.

8% Not concerned at all.

*

How concerned would you be about catching an STD?

54% Extremely concerned; I'd feel like my life was basically over.

31% Very concerned; I wouldn't be able to think about anything else.

6% Concerned, but I'd recover.

2% A little concerned.

7% Not concerned at all.

"I have a very serious question. I liked this guy that was overage and we talked and made out and stuff like that. Well, my dad didn't think it was okay, just because of his age. That didn't stop me from seeing this boy. We had sex and I didn't tell anyone about it. I became preg-nant. Then we had sex again and he told everyone about it and made me out to be a slut. I lost the baby to miscarriage. I was wondering if I should tell my dad or anyone else about it. I think that they would freak and try to press charges, and I love my boyfriend too much to al-low that. What should I do? Thank you."   —Maura, 14, Minnesota

This letter was sent to me by a 14-year-old girl who only knew me from the Letter to Teens on my website. This note really exemplifies why having these conversations is so important and why all parents need to take specific steps to stay in their teenager's life and try to influence their choices. This girl's dad already knows she's in over her head, dating someone too old, and he probably suspects she's moving along faster sexually than she's ready to. He's talked to her and told her to slow down and stop seeing this guy he doesn't like.

She's even savvy enough to know that her "boyfriend" could get charged with statutory rape if their relationship is revealed. (When teens say "overage" it tends to mean either over 18 or over 21, in ei-ther case upsetting—not to mention illegal—as a sex partner for a 14-year-old.) Nonetheless, she's gotten pregnant, is scared to tell her father about it, and is still in love with this older guy who, from her own account, sounds like a jerk at best. How sad that she seems so afraid of simply talking to her own dad.

It's true that teen pregnancy in the United States is down and that teens are having less sex and using more contraception. However, now is no time to be complacent about these statistics. First and fore-most, even if there is only *one* unwanted teen pregnancy in the United States, that's one too many, especially for that particular teen's family. There are other vital reasons to start talking more candidly and openly about pregnancy and STDs with teenagers today:

STD PREVENTION IS A TOUGH SELL TO TEENS

Teens often engage in "magical thinking," meaning that, even if you tell a teenager how many teens get STDs each year, they will think, *That won't happen to me.* It's not that teens are contrary; it's simply how they think. This thinking is reinforced by the fact that STDs (including chlamydia and HPV) can remain symptomless, at times for years—especially in boys. Because of this, even though it is often reported that as many as 1 in 4 teens will contract an STD at some point (and that as many as 9 million teenagers and young adults got STDs in the year 2000 alone), the real number of young people that catch STDs each year may be even higher because those who have no symptoms may not seek medical attention.

But symptomless does not in any way equal harmless. A boy can carry chlamydia for years without symptoms, then pass it to a girl who may have no symptoms for years but could eventually develop a full-blown case of pelvic inflammatory disease as a result and be rendered infertile. And of course there are the dangers of AIDS, which can also lie dormant for a long time before showing symptoms.

A lot of teens will say that they start off using condoms with their partner but after a few months they feel it's a sign of commitment and trust to stop using them. Unfortunately, if one or both partners has sex outside the relationship, or was already carrying an STD from a past relationship, then the STD gets transmitted once again. Teens also often say they don't want to use condoms because they know their partner is "clean"—but in most cases this declaration of "clean-ness" is based on the teen's perception of their partner's present and past behavior, non on a clean bill of health from a doctor.

"I didn't use protection—I was in love"

"I was 14 when I started having sex and I was careful. The key word in that sentence is *was*. The two times I did not use protection . . . I was in love. I trusted them. Little did I know I should have either gone to a clinic with them to get checked out together or used protection.

"At first, I thought I had an allergic reaction to soap. So I told my mom that I needed to go to the doctor; I didn't say why. When I got there I was so nervous. I was in the room, sitting on that little uncomfortable table naked. The doctor examined me and knew right away what it was. He told me, 'You have the STD herpes. Would you like me to tell your mom?'

"I was trying so hard to hold my feelings in and replied, 'Yes.' He left the room and I broke down. My mom came in and just hugged me as she started to cry, too. I felt like nothing mattered now. My mom and I started talking, which was good because I felt worthless and I needed someone to keep telling me it will be all right. I was so embarrassed. I didn't want anyone to know that I had an STD that I'll never get rid of.

"I try to talk to my little sister, but she has the same attitude I did. I'm hoping that my story actually catches people's attention and shows them you have to be careful and don't always believe word of mouth. You can only trust yourself because you can't lie to you."   —Trista, 19, Kentucky

To impress a feeling of urgency upon high school students, some sex ed. classes show horrific slides of "STDs gone wild," which can serve as a deterrent to unprotected sex (or any sex, for that matter). It's easy to convince a teen that they don't want their genitalia to morph into a disease-ridden painful mass of tissue. But the results of such scare tactics, while effective and lasting for some teens, can be short-lived for others. It doesn't take long for some teens to rationalize that it's highly unlikely that they'll get an extreme case of herpes or warts that would go untreated for years until their bodies resembled those in the pictures. Even the threat of AIDS is no longer as frightening to young people as it once was. AIDS is now viewed by many teens as a manageable disease, something that is bad to have but can be treated with medication. "People that are becoming sexually active now didn't live through the '80s, so they didn't see what guys look like as they were wasting away from an HIV infection," says family nurse practitioner Rosemary Prentice. "Now it's thought of as kind of like a chronic disease, like high blood pressure. They don't know anybody whose pills haven't worked; they never saw the horror of HIV, so to them it's not a big deal." And besides, they think, none of their friends have contracted AIDS or had STDs that looked like the ones in the pictures. And those few friends who have contracted STDs, teens reason, took a dose of penicillin and cleared it right up.

✳ Misconceptions Teens Have About STDs ✳

25% of surveyed teens age 15 to 17 agree that if someone they were
dating had an STD they would know.
20% agree that STDs can only be spread when
symptoms are present.
12% agree that "unless you have had sex with a lot of people, STDs are
not something you have to worry about."
10% agree that "STDs are a nuisance, but they do not have
any serious health effects."
—Kaiser Family Foundation, 2003

It is hard to convince teens to be worried about something they can't see or feel. "There's a lot of ignorance about STIs," says Michaeline Rittenman, a family nurse practitioner at Planned Parenthood in New York. "Many think if you have oral intercourse you're safe from STIs" (which isn't true). "And," Rittenman adds, "there's still a lot of 'it can't happen to me' going on." That's why the "Real-World Advice" section of this chapter has tips for making STDs feel less hypothetical and more like immediate dangers.

✳ **Exclusive National Survey Results** ✳
Teens: Tell the Truth!

Who would you talk to first about catching an STD?

56% a parent

14% a friend

13% don't know

6% a sibling

5% another trusted adult

4% boyfriend or girlfriend

1% clergy

1% teacher

TEENS HAVE DIFFICULTY PLANNING

As mentioned in detail in Chapter 4, teens on the whole are not great at planning. This is never more unfortunate than when it comes to the issue of STD and pregnancy prevention, which require not only careful planning, but complex, coordinated planning on the part of two teenagers. As one parent says, "I can't get a commitment of whether my kids are going to be around for dinnertime tomorrow night—that level of planning they're not willing to do, because what if something good comes up in between today and tomorrow night?"

The idea of planning is especially important for teenagers who want to choose abstinence, because making the abstract decision to be abstinent is very different from actually choosing abstinence in the heat of the moment. "Teens who say their method of not getting pregnant or not getting an infection is abstinence don't plan to have sex. And so they don't have anything with them. They don't have condoms; and then it *just happens*," says HiTOPs' director of educational programs Elizabeth Casparian, Ph.D.

There's that phrase again. Any time sex "just happens" to teens, they are at increased risk of contracting an STD or ending up with an unwanted pregnancy.

I listened when my parents said:

"Do you want to give up your youth? Because we will *not* baby-sit for you."

—Girl, 14, Mississippi

TEENS VIEW TEEN PREGNANCY AS A PROBLEM *ADULTS* MUST HELP SOLVE

Teens who mention teen pregnancy as being a problem at their school often express a feeling of frustration, as in: *Isn't anyone going to do anything about this*? A National Campaign to Prevent Teen Pregnancy study found that 63 percent of teens surveyed agree that parents are most responsible for fixing the problem of teen pregnancy. Teens sometimes tell me their suggestions for helping the situation such as (different kinds of sex ed. or parents getting more involved). And those who bring up the issue of teen pregnancy often cite the exact number of pregnancies at their school—showing they are very aware of this as a problem, even when they themselves are not directly affected.

"We have 12 pregnant girls at our school"

"I go to high school in a small town—we have 12 pregnant girls at our school. It is a bad deal. I would say that probably about two out of the 350 kids in our school wanted to get pregnant. Those two kids are doing it on purpose, but the others definitely are not. I have no idea if these pregnant girls were practicing safe sex or not. But obviously you can't rely on birth control or condoms.

"It is a big problem because kids don't realize what they are getting themselves into, and usually the kid won't have a great life because the parents are not mature enough. If parents want to communicate with their kids, they have to initiate the conversation because I still don't talk to my mom about my girlfriends or what I did this weekend or any of that unless she talks to me, and usually when she talks to me about it I feel comfortable with her. Parents need to keep their eye on their kids and have talks about it."

—Jamie, 15, Iowa

"Better sex ed. would help"

"There is an unusually high number of pregnant girls at my school, twenty-two. This great number upsets me. I feel that better sexual education would've prevented such a high pregnancy rate. The only information that is provided about sex in our health class is have no sex at all; information is left out, leaving us to make decisions for ourselves, which most of the time isn't the best choice. Through friends or TV we learn little suggestions on how to be safe and be smart. I am smart about my actions and take the appropriate actions to ensure my safety and health, but unfortunately, not many people do the same."   —Rachelle, 17, Pennsylvania

When teens don't talk about how to prevent pregnancy and STDs with an adult they trust, they, like Rachelle, are often left to come up with their own ideas about how to do so.

✳ What makes teens use or not use ✳ contraception?

• Teens who talked to their partners about contraception before sex had more than twice the likelihood of ever using contraception than those who did not discuss it.

• For each month a teenager delayed first sex after the start of a romantic relationship, the likelihood of consistent contraceptive use increased by 5 percent.

- Teens who dated older partners had a lower likelihood of consistent contraceptive use.

- For each year a partner was older than the respondent, the likelihood of always using contraception decreased by 11 percent.

- Teens who had taken a virginity pledge were 57 percent less likely to always use contraception than those who had not taken a pledge.

- Teens who used a combination of at least two contraceptive methods had a much higher likelihood of being consistent contraceptive users than those who used only one method or who varied between single and multiple methods.

—Child Trends, 2004

I listened when my parents said:
"Look at the negative financial effects of getting pregnant early."

—Boy, 12, Connecticut

TEENS ARE SCARED TO ASK PARENTS FOR BIRTH CONTROL

If a teen wants to use birth control that's not available at a drugstore, he or she will likely need a parent's help, and that can serve as a major obstacle to getting birth control into that teen's hands. Though teens can go to Planned Parenthood or other clinics that provide services on a sliding-scale fee or for free, many simply don't have the transportation or wherewithal to navigate this process on their own. With or without good reason, many teens say they don't want to ask their parents to help them get birth control because they're afraid their parents will assume (or know) that they're sexually active.

"Teens don't want their parents to know they are having sex"

"Some of the sexually active teens I know use birth control, but it's very few of them. Some don't have money to buy birth control pills or they are scared and ashamed to tell their parents that they need birth control pills because they don't want their parents knowing that they are having sex.

"I couldn't go to my parents to ask questions about sex because one: I didn't feel comfortable, and two: my mom and I don't have the relationship where I can talk about anything without having my head bit off. I learned from music, TV shows and friends. I would go on information sites and look up stuff, too.

"When I got pregnant I wasn't on any kind of birth control. I didn't know where to get birth control, I didn't know how much it would cost, and I didn't want to go to my parents about it because I was too ashamed to let them know that I needed it because I was now having sex.

"My advice to parents about birth control is don't always assume that if someone needs birth control, they are automatically sexually active. Some girls I know are virgins and on birth control.

"I will be more open with my daughter. I'll let her know the consequences of what she does decide to do. I don't want to preach to her, 'don't do it, don't do it,' because that makes kids want to do it more. That's how it was in my case. In my religion you're not supposed to do that until you're married. I got tired of hearing it, and I wanted to rebel one time—to see if I could do it."

—Vera, 18, Indiana

✳ Exclusive National Survey Results ✳
Teens: Tell the Truth!

Whose responsibility is it to be sure a couple uses birth control?
85% Both partners take equal responsibility.
5% The girl's.

2% The guy's.

6% Don't know.

2 percent I don't believe in birth control.

"She wasn't on the Pill . . . we rarely used a condom"

"It all started sophomore year in high school. I noticed a girl who always sat in the back like me. She seemed to look at me a lot. So we started to talk and got to be friends. I asked her out, and she said yes. The next few months were pretty much like any other high school relationship. Then we decided to take it to the next level. That was an amazing night; it was the first time for both us. From there it turned serious. This girl was my life. I can't even explain how I felt about her. We had some bad fights, which only made us stronger I think. Then it finally happened: she got pregnant. As I look back I'm surprised that it did not happen sooner. She was not on the Pill; we very rarely used a condom. The day she went to get the pregnancy test I was unable to go because my mother had grounded me. Later my mother said all I had to do was tell her my girlfriend was getting a pregnancy test. Well you try telling your parents something like this. That would be hard for you, too.

"So I'm sitting at home and the phone rings. I will never forget this call, from my girlfriend. She says 'I'm pregnant.' She was crying. I will never forget her voice, I was so scared, she was more scared than me. So I told her to come to my house to talk. As I got off the phone I sat down with my mom and told her everything that was happening. My girlfriend got there, and we called her parents and my dad to all come over. I was scared to death to see her parents. I was like a part of their family, and I had gotten their daughter pregnant. I can't even imagine what was going through their minds.

"We decided to have an abortion—I was so young. There is no way to explain the amount of regret I have and will always have. I can't explain the feelings I get when looking at a baby. After she got the abortion, soon after, we broke up. At this point in my life I did a lot of growing up and a lot of thinking. After losing her it is safe to say I actually loved her and I knew the feeling of love after all."

—Julian, 18, New Mexico

Though health-care providers at various clinics tell me that parents sometimes come in with teens, this scenario is often talked about as the rare exception to the rule, which is teens who find their way on their own, with friends, or with their boyfriend or girlfriend. If a teen is responsible enough to take control of her health care, this isn't necessarily a bad thing, but then again I have heard from many teens who, despite their doctor's very clear warnings against it, didn't think it was a big deal to smoke while taking birth control pills. While some teens are mature enough to get information from a doctor and follow directions, others may be too intimidated (by even the nicest of doctors) or may need assistance navigating these complex health decisions and interpreting medical information.

REAL-WORLD ADVICE

I don't think I need to spend a lot of ink motivating you to convince your teenager that an unwanted pregnancy or STD would likely have a negative impact on his or her life. The goal of talking to your teen about pregnancy and STDs are 1) to help your teen understand that pregnancy and STDs are a very real risk and to motivate her to be prepared in a very real way to face that risk head-on before becoming sexually active, and 2) to make absolutely certain that your teen knows and understands the mechanics and practicalities of preventing unwanted pregnancy and sexually transmitted diseases, from which birth control methods are safest to how to actually use those methods every time she has sex.

BECOME A SEX-EDUCATED PARENT

To speak intelligently with your teen about sexual health, you don't need to know the latest advances in the Pill or the exact efficacy of various types of condoms. But wouldn't it be great if you did? There are several advantages to educating yourself on the various types of birth control and STD-prevention methods available. Just learning this material will make you feel more comfortable and confident talking about it. It's empowering to know that you are making yourself a trusted source of accurate information for your teen, and your teenager will sense that you know what you're talking about, which will make him or her more inclined to ask you questions that deal with all aspects of sex.

This book offers many *national* statistics and jumping-off points for conversation. To get a grasp on what's happening in your community, says Kathleen Ethier, Ph.D., behavioral scientist in the division of sexually transmitted disease prevention at the CDC, call your state health department and find out about local STD rates and teen birth rates. To find your state health department, just type "[your state] State Health Department" into a search engine. Some of the websites even have these facts and figures online.

TIP: For easy (and visual) guides to the basics, invest in copies of Robie Harris's books *It's Perfectly Normal* and *It's So Amazing.* They're meant for younger kids but are great resources for any age.

Also find sex Q&As, particularly for girls, in *The Seventeen Guide to Sex and Your Body* (which I wrote).

Go to your own doctor and ask her about the latest and most effective birth control and STD-prevention methods that are best for teens. Check out the questions and answers on sites like teenpregnancy.org, teenwire.com, and Sex, Etc. (sxetc.org). If you're

Talk the Talk: Teenagers Will Listen if You Say...

"You know there are a lot of myths about how you can get pregnant or catch an STD. I once heard that you can't get pregnant the first time, which isn't true—you *can* get pregnant the first time you have sex. And you can also catch STDs from oral sex. Have you ever heard something and thought *That can't be true?* If you ever want to check something out with me, to find out if it's true or not, I'll get you the correct information so you always know the real deal."

"Can you name four kinds of birth control methods? Try to find the answers, and let's talk once you have some notes, okay? I know this is like homework! But it's important that you really understand this stuff and that I *know* you understand it, so look at this as a pop quiz." If you feel uncomfortable springing this on your teen out loud, pass a note under their door. Or e-mail them this question. Let your teenager look up answers on the web, which will give you an opportunity to go over reliable versus unreliable sites, as well as discuss the various benefits of each kind of method. "Which method do you think is the easiest to use? Which one is the simplest to be sure it's used every single time?" Talking in the abstract takes it away from "you're going to use this when you have sex," which will make the conversation easier on you while making your teenager think about what is possible and what is practical.

a mother, don't just get the stats and facts on the Pill; ask the doctor the questions you'd want the answers to ("Which pill is most likely to clear up skin and least likely to make you gain weight?"). If you're a dad, be sure you can explain how to use a condom. If it's been a long time since you last reviewed the timing and logistics of the whole sperm-egg phenomenon, whip out your old pregnancy books and review.

It sounds like a lot of work, and it is, but look at it this way: if your teen told you he wanted to travel to a foreign land, you'd find out what shots he needed and be sure he was able to get clean water and protect against malaria, right? This is the same thing. Laura Gauld of the Hyde Schools, who is one of the most innovative and dedicated parents I've ever talked to, says, "Good parenting is always inconvenient for the parent." This is a great example of that theory in action.

Every teen is going to be driven, at some point, to seek out this information. There are lots of great places for teens to get sound advice about sex and contraception, including the websites mentioned in this book, their school's nurse or health teacher, or a clinic. But there are also many unreliable sources of information, including but not limited to their friends, random websites, and even some well-intentioned but misinformed adults. There are a lot of myths about sex and contraception that sound credible to teens. Not everyone is comfortable dispensing this kind of information to their teenager, but if you have the information in your arsenal, at the very least you'll be in a position to tell your teenager if something he holds to be true is in fact true—or dangerously false.

TIP: "Even if we don't ask, we still have questions." This is just one point in The National Campaign to Prevent Teen Pregnancy's PDF "Talking Back: What Teens Want Adults to Know About Teen Pregnancy." Download it as well as "Parent Power" at www.teenpregnancy.org, and use them as guides to start a discussion.

BE SURE YOUR TEEN UNDERSTANDS PREGNANCY
IN A CONCRETE WAY

Teenagers often think of STDs and teen pregnancy in a hypothetical way, so it's your challenge to make these risks feel very immediate and real, before they *are* very immediate and real. Marisa Nightingale, senior director of media programs and youth initiatives at The National Campaign to Prevent Teen Pregnancy, feels that a combination of straight talk and positivity with a dash of cold reality thrown in may be the most effective way to communicate these important messages: "Some people would say that we should only show positive messages about sex to young people; others would say that showing consequences is the only thing that will aid in prevention. I personally believe that you have to do a little bit of both—and no matter what your message is it has to feel real, and not preachy."

This was absolutely reflected in responses given by the teens surveyed for this book. When asked what their parents said that impacted them the most, a good deal of them cited "scary" messages like "Having a baby will kill your future" and "You're playing Russian roulette with your life." Others cited positive statements like, "Maintaining virginity protects my body," "Respect the other person and yourself," and, simply, "They said that I am special."

TIP: Give your teen a choice: "Do you want to talk about this now or later?" You still get to bring it up, but she'll feel a little more in control.

The more honest and direct you are about these topics, the more your teen may decide for himself that he's not ready to face these risks and may decide to wait a while, until he's more mature, to begin having sex. In any case, the more concrete and real you can make the risk of pregnancy feel, the more likely it will resonate with your teen enough for him to take action to prevent it.

Talk the Talk: Teenagers Will Listen if You Say...

"Let's talk about pregnancy for a minute, because whenever you have sex, which I assume you will someday, you risk pregnancy—no birth control method is 100 percent effective. So let's play this out for a minute. Your girlfriend calls, and she took a home pregnancy test. It's positive. What would you do?" Let your teen come up with his own answer without rushing in. Your goal is to get him thinking about this for himself, not to feed him a scenario he'll feel is unlikely or "just you freaking." Whatever his answer is, follow the analogy to its logical end. For example, if he says, "I'd take responsibility and marry her and raise the child," you can say, "Okay, let's play that out: where will you two live? And how will you make money? And who will watch the child while you're working? What if there are medical complications with the baby—or what if the girl decides that she wants to give *you* full custody because this is all too much for her to deal with? What would you do?" You may discover that your teen has some faulty ideas about how much things cost—or how involved you would be willing to be with his hypothetical child.

Even though this conversation will likely make you feel agitated as you imagine your teen making decisions that you feel may be wrong (or "ruining his life"), the key is to say all this in a very *calm* way and help your teen to figure out for himself what the reality of life with baby would be like. The minute you start yelling or making your teen feel stupid is the minute your teen shuts down and decides you don't, after all, understand anything and all this is so far-fetched and won't happen anyway so why are you bumming him out? You want to make your teen feel that you're putting him in control of his life and empowering him to make smart choices, not like he's defending himself against your attacks.

To get started, help your teen imagine what it would be like to be pregnant or to get someone pregnant. Use as specific language as you can to really paint a picture for your teenager, and don't shy away from asking tough questions, in a nonconfrontational way, to get your teen thinking. For instance, if the teen says, "Oh, I'd give the baby up for adoption," you can remind her of other children she's close to or even pets she's loved—can she imagine parting with them? Tell her (if you know) what it feels like to be pregnant (or to get someone you love pregnant) and how you felt when your baby was born. Use any examples or analogies you think will have an impact on your teenager, and really get her to think about the possible outcomes.

TIP: Tell boys that if they get a girl pregnant, the boy may have no say over what the girl decides to do about the pregnancy. If the girl decides to raise the baby, the boy may be responsible for child-support payments (as well as emotional support) for that child for the rest of his life. Add up the dollars so it feels real.

MAKE STD RISK FEEL CONCRETE

A similar tactic will work when you're discussing STDs; help your teen live with the idea of what her life would be like if she were to contract an STD. The statistics in these chapters are meant to help you understand how many teens are affected by these issues, but you can also use them to help your teen understand that she is by no means immune. If one in four teens catches an STD, remind your teen, for instance, that there are four teens in your soccer carpool—one of them could be that "one in four."

Talk the Talk: Teenagers Will Listen if You Say...

"I want us to talk about sexually transmitted diseases, even though this is kind of an awkward thing to talk about, it's so important that I want us to discuss it. STDs are transmitted via unprotected sex, and even if you are guarding against them by using condoms, condoms are not 100 percent effective. So it's important to know that if you have sex, you're risking STDs, including permanent ones, like HIV and herpes. A lot of people don't know this, but you often can't tell if someone has an STD just by looking at them. A person can have chlamydia, or even herpes, or HIV, and not show it. What would you do if you thought you'd contracted an STD? How would you take care of yourself? Let's say you found out you have herpes . . . every time you have a new partner, you'll need to tell that person about the STD . . . what would you say? How would you bring it up? In what ways would having an STD get in the way of you living the life you hope to lead?"

Again, the idea is not to drum up hysteria in the teenager or make him feel that if he does get an STD, all is lost and his life is over. This is especially important because it's entirely possible that some parents will delve into this topic, take their teen to the doctor, and discover that the teenager is already in fact carrying an STD. Rather, the point is to help him grasp the many ways that contracting an STD can change his life, today and in the future.

I listened when my parents said:

"You have too much going for you to end up with a child—or an STD. Don't you want to go off to college and pursue your dreams and goals?"

—Girl, 15, Kentucky

BE SURE TEENS KNOW HOW TO PROTECT THEMSELVES

Even if your wishes for your teen are that she abstain from sex until marriage and you are confident she feels the same way, it's important to remember that some teens—not all but some—will tell parents what they want to hear, so you can't completely trust that your teen's word is her oath on this one. Even if a teen is staunchly opposed to having sex before she gets married, things happen. Situations change, and so can her mind. It's far, far better for her to have this information and not need it, than to need it and not have it. And for reasons discussed in Chapter 6, please don't rely on sex ed. class to fully educate her in this realm. Sex ed. is a great resource, but view it as supplemental information, even if the school has a fantastic program. Consider the damage if she misses the day they discuss condoms or has band practice during the pregnancy lesson.

The primary weapon a teen needs to protect against pregnancy and STDs is a *plan*. Whether it's a plan for how to say no (see Chapter 3 for a detailed talk about this) or a plan to use a certain kind of birth control, doesn't matter—as long as it's a clearly articulated plan. And she needs a backup plan. What if she says no but her date continues to pressure her? What if the condom breaks? What if she forgets to take her birth control pill? And this is key: the teenager must be committed to implementing the plan every single time they have sex.

"One of the core messages we've been giving to teens since the day we began is: Have A Plan," says Marisa Nightingale, senior director of media programs and youth initiatives at The National Campaign to Prevent Teen Pregnancy. "The plan can be to say no. But if you say no—are you worried about hurt feelings? If the plan is to use contraception—where will you get it? Whatever the plan is, teens need to think it through before they're in the moment, because once they're in the moment, it's really tough."

So the task is to first be sure your teen understands and has easy access to the birth control options that are available to her. The easiest way to do this is to call a center such as Planned Parenthood and

Talk the Talk: Teenagers Will Listen if You Say...

"If you're going to have sex, and I hope you won't have sex until you're [your goal for your teen here], you need to look out for your body and your health. You are the most important thing in my life, and I wouldn't be doing my job if I didn't tell you that having sex has risks and those risks scare me because I hate the idea of anything bad happening to you. So we're going to go to [the doctor, Planned Parenthood, your local clinic—you have called in advance and spoken to this agency to be sure they have the materials and wherewithal to discuss birth control and STD prevention intelligently and thoroughly with your teen]. Because I want to be sure you understand how to protect yourself against STDs and pregnancy.

"You can talk to the doctor without me there, and she won't tell me what you tell her so please be honest. And if you do decide to become sexually active, you need to visit this doctor in advance [for girls—or you can say "with your girlfriend" for boys] to get birth control. Of course, no birth control or STD-prevention method is 100 percent effective; that's why you need to use two methods. This is one of those times when close won't cut it—you need to use two methods, every single time you have sex."

ask if they have workshops or someone who could talk to your teen about the different birth control and STD-prevention options. Then remember that the plan won't work if your teen can't accomplish it fairly easily and consistently. Go to the local drugstore and look for where they keep the condoms. Are they behind the counter so the teen has to ask the pharmacist, or are they out in the open? If your teen won't feel comfortable asking for condoms (or can't afford them), you can find out how he can get them for free, buy them yourself, or help him find a store where they're accessible. Are you sure your teen understands the difference between lambskin (not effective against

AIDS prevention) and latex condoms? Don't let your teen off the hook with "I'll use condoms"—really talk about the plan until all the details are clear and the plan seems very doable. This is not the same as giving your teen permission to have sex. You're still communicating your goals and hopes for your teenager. But remember that someday he will be sexually active—and by then it'll be too late to start educating him.

TIP: Before each conversation, try to pause for a moment and get inside your teen's head. What might he be thinking? What might he be afraid to tell you? What might she be afraid you're going to think?

After the doctor's appointment, follow up with your teen (you might give her a few days to absorb so she doesn't feel bombarded). Find out what her plan is and how she is going to stay committed to her plan every single time. This is easier if your teen isn't sexually active yet. Role play. You be the partner and say things like "I hate using condoms; they feel gross." If you don't feel comfortable doing that, then just list things guys say to get out of using condoms (if you're a woman, these will be easy enough to recall; if you're a man, hopefully you have to ask your wife for this list). Let your teen show you that she's committed to keeping herself safe.

This is an awkward conversation, no doubt about it, because to have it correctly, both you and your teen have to at least imagine a scenario where it might be possible that your teen is going to have sex. But even though this is hard to do, it's important to go over your teen's plan not just once but periodically, to be sure that as new pressures and influences and ideas emerge, her plan either stays intact or evolves to something equally protective and intelligent.

During one of these early "protect yourself" conversations is a good time to remind your teen of the old saying "If you can't talk about something, you're not ready to do it." Teens who talk about birth control with their partners are far more likely to actually use it.

If you're having trouble getting started with this conversation, you can photocopy the following cheat sheet and have your teen fill it out. Please note that even if your teen's plan is to choose abstinence, he or she still needs to have a plan in place to be sure they stick to that choice.

The Plan: To Stay Safe from STDs and Unwanted Pregnancy

- **What's my plan to stay safe from STDs?**

- **What's my plan to avoid getting pregnant or getting someone pregnant?**

- **How will I enact each part of my plan? (Be very specific.)**

- **How can I prepare for "the moment" way in advance of "the moment"?**

- **How can I practice my plan in advance of "the moment"?**

- **How can I be sure my plan will work every single time?**

It's up to you if you want your teen to share his answers with you or just know that he's done this exercise to get him thinking in the right direction. But if you do have him share, it gives you the opportunity to help him think of circumstances he might not consider—like if his plan is abstinence, how will he feel if some of his close friends start talking about having sex and how great it is? Or if her plan involves condoms, where will she buy them and how will she talk to her partner about using them? Again, there's more than one way to have a difficult conversation; if you're squeamish talking about it over the dinner table, your teen can e-mail you answers or IM you or leave you a note—you don't get points taken away for lack of style here, it's substance that matters.

OTHER STEPS TO HELP TEENS AVOID UNWANTED PREGNANCY

There are certain characteristics shared by all teen-pregnancy-prevention programs that have been proven to work, and they are principles that can be applied to any teen to help them avoid unwanted pregnancy. These programs tend to be comprehensive, and there's usually a reliable adult supervising who cares deeply about the kids in the program. There's generally an aspect to the program where the teens feel a part of something larger than themselves; they feel that they are part of a community in which they play an important role.

"I have a sign in my office that says 'Teen Pregnancy Is Not Okay,'" says Sarah Brown, director of The National Campaign to Prevent Teen Pregnancy. "The teenage years need to be for education and growing up and having fun. They are not for early pregnancy and parenthood and heavy responsibilities and expenses. These basic value statements really make a difference."

Sometimes pregnancy-prevention programs include job training; sometimes they simply occupy the teenagers' time in a constructive way that enhances their self-esteem. High expectations are set for the teen, and she is held accountable for meeting those expectations. "It's not just about communication," says Kathleen Ethier, Ph.D., a behavioral scientist in the division of STD prevention at the CDC. "Though that's very important, it's about having them in a supervised environment after school and monitoring their day-to-day activities—we know for a fact that this trio makes a huge difference in the teens' behavior. Kids whose parents know where they are, who they're with, and what they're doing, are kids who are less likely to have sex early and more likely to use protection when they do have sex."

Teens are taught that they are valued and can achieve success and be a part of something important, something that has nothing to do with how they look or whether they have a boyfriend or girlfriend.

Most of all, the teens are made to feel that they matter and that their future is important. "Young people need to have a community and a sense of identity and purpose," says Michael Resnick, Ph.D., director of the National Teen Pregnancy Prevention Research Center and director of the Healthy Youth Development Prevention Research Center at the University of Minnesota. "When young people have opportunities for fun and engagement and contribution, when they feel like they've got a future and they know a pathway to get there, these are kids who have every reason to say, I've got so much going on right now. Pregnancy is okay for someday, but not now."

You don't have to enroll your teen in a program that is specifically intended to keep them from being pregnant or getting someone pregnant, but do consider making sure your teenager is invested in something beyond his everyday schoolwork and friends—whether it's a music program or volunteering. Anything that keeps him focused on his role in this world and his bright future ahead will help him more easily internalize the importance of avoiding pregnancy.

TIP: Watch how you talk about other kids, even TV-show characters, and their decisions. If you say a teen who has sex or gets pregnant is a total idiot, you're sending the message, "Don't come to me if this happens to you."

PREPARE FOR THE "WORST-CASE SCENARIO"

Only 47 percent of the teens in the Tell the Truth! survey would tell a parent first about being pregnant. Unfortunately, when a pregnancy occurs, some decisions need to be made very quickly—for instance if a condom breaks and a girl wants to take emergency contraception (EC), she has 72 hours to take the first dose for it to be up to 89 percent effective.

Talk the Talk: Teenagers Will Listen if You Say...

"I know that you know I'd be sad, and even disappointed, if you were to get pregnant [get someone pregnant] or contract an STD. I might even be angry—but I would move past that anger and all those feelings to help you, because you're what's most important to me. If you have any major health or sexuality issue, I hope you would always come to me right away so I could help you manage the situation. I would always look out for your health and well-being, first and foremost, and I would want to help you, and take care of you."

TIP: The emergency contraception hotline, which can advise on where EC is available, is 1-888-NOT2LATE. Or log on to www.not-2-late.com.

If something as dramatic as pregnancy happens to your teen, you want to be in on this news as early as possible so you can help them make the best decisions. So the goal here is to be sure your teen knows, that even though you've just spent time telling her you feel extremely strongly that she do everything in her power not to get pregnant or contract an STD, you of course want her to come to you right away with a problem of this magnitude. Say this as clearly as possible, because the last thing you want is for your teen to be making decisions about something this important on her own or with only her same-age friends as support and resources.

THE LAST WORD

It's so awful to think about your teenager getting pregnant or getting someone pregnant, or contracting any kind of STD, that these topics are very hard to talk about. But talking about these issues is the one way to actually help prevent them. Think of the letter at the beginning of this chapter when you feel uncomfortable bringing something up or you're tempted to avoid the topic because you don't think your teenager wants to talk to you. It's entirely possible that your teen, like the teen who wrote that letter, *does* want to hear from you, even about these really difficult topics. More importantly, your teen *needs* to talk with you about them.

The **Conversation** Continues . . .

The best part of any job is having people say "thank you." It's a shame that we live in somewhat of a thankless society, where many people think the way to drive people to work harder is to reserve that "thank you" so no one gets too complacent or stops trying. It's too bad because, in my experience, when people say thank you, it makes all the difference in how you feel about your life, your work, and your life's work.

In this way, I'm extremely lucky because I am in a position where the most important people in the world—your teenagers—thank me every day. I get notes almost every day from teens, saying thank you for writing me back; thank you for reading my letter; thank you for interviewing me; thank you for helping me have a voice in this world; thank you for giving me information so I could make smart choices; or thank you, what you wrote changed the way I see things. And the mama of all thank-yous: thank you—what you said changed my life.

Although I love getting the thanks, I don't believe all this thanking is because I have some special way of relating to teens. I think what teens are reacting to is the fact that they know I want to listen to them and talk with them, and they can tell I care about them. They know this in part because I often come right out and say "I want to talk to you" or "I want to hear from you." That simple gesture connects with teenagers who so often feel marginalized and ignored, stuck in that "too old for trick-or-treating, too young to vote" limbo. They don't get a say in terms of where they live, what school they go to, or whether or not they can drive or come and go when they please or buy many of the things that they want.

But there are some things in their control, and sex is one of those things. Having a boyfriend or girlfriend is not only fun and a thrilling experience—it also makes them feel powerful in many ways. Having a boyfriend or girlfriend will also get a teen plenty of parental attention as well—one way or another. And it gives them someone to share all their secrets with. Someone, in some cases, to create some new secrets with as well.

GETTING TEENS TO SHARE THEIR SECRETS

Teens often tell me they're going to reveal something to me that they could "never tell their parents." Remember what teens say when I ask how their parents or other concerned adults would react to the truth?

"They'd freak out."
"They'd kick me out of the house."
"They wouldn't understand."
"They don't know what it's like to be a teenager now."

Preempt these arguments, which are almost always patently false. Say, "Maybe I don't know what it's like to be a teenager now. So tell me. I'm listening to you. I want to hear from you. I want to talk to you. I won't freak out." Of course, this only works if you can show your teenager that you truly do want to listen, and you need as well to make a concerted effort, no matter how much what your teen says makes you feel anxious (or even angry), not to freak out.

But even if you do freak out (let's face it, some of what teens have to say these days can be freakout-worthy) all isn't lost, because this isn't a onetime conversation. It's an ongoing dialogue that you've earned by creating an atmosphere of open communication and truth-telling in your household. You always have the opportunity to go back to your teen and say, "Okay, I freaked out the last time we talked about this. Let's talk about it like adults now."

THERE ARE MANY WAYS TO CONNECT WITH TEENS

There's no one right way to have these talks. The important thing is to have them and to keep having them. I'm actually a little shy. I like to e-mail back and forth with teens or talk on the phone with them. Maybe you like writing letters, too, or e-mailing, or keeping a family journal in a central place that everyone can write in.

However you do it, conversing with your teenager will have an enormous impact on her, as long as you're making the effort to be clear about your expectations, yet respectful of the fact that your teen is an individual with her own stresses and choices to make. Don't trivialize her feelings or refer to things as "a phase," even if you honestly suspect that's true. She's too old for this kind of language, and you'll put a stop to open communication. Be respectful of how much information your teenager can handle at any one sitting, and for goodness' sake, don't go all out all at once to have some marathon conversation that'll make him want to avoid you in the kitchen for weeks to come until he perceives that you're off of your "talking about sex" kick. Multiple, smaller conversations filled with plenty of questions on your part are most likely to yield desirable results.

But here's the catch: talking is just the first part.

GETTING AND STAYING INVOLVED

Teens look kind of like adults, and they definitely want to be treated like adults, so it can be hard to remember that they are in fact still children who very much want and need your guidance. One shift that can be particularly hard to navigate is from being their primary information source and go-to answer person, to more of an "adviser" role. In other words, they used to take your advice as gospel, and now you have to convince them that your advice is more worth listening to than the sound of the din around them.

THE POWER OF RESPECT

The best way to do this is to use the one thing that teens want most and get least: respect. Every time you ask your teen a question and remember the details from your last conversation, you're showing that you have respect for them and their choices, their friends, and everything that's important to them. When your teen wants to do something that seems stupid or unsafe, don't dismiss them with a simple "no." Find out who else will be there and why this is so important. You can still say no, but your teen will see that you've made an effort to see their point of view, which is respectful. Allow your teen to express himself or herself through poetry or song or any other creative means that speaks to them, without judging their efforts. Show an interest in whatever they are interested in. Learn the lyrics to his favorite song. Let your teen teach you about how things are at their school, about math, about life. You don't always have to know more than your teenager. Sometimes allowing your teen to be the one who knows more, or is right, or is the interesting one at the dinner table, is the most respectful thing you can do.

Teens translate "you respect me" into "you care about me for me," and that is a very valuable relationship builder. Teens who feel their parents respect them are the ones who tell me they are open, honest, and happy with the relationship they have with their parents. They're also far more likely to go to their parents for help when they truly need it—and more importantly, they come to their parents for help *before* an emergency arises.

BE A PART OF THE VILLAGE

Teens who make smart decisions are also usually the ones whose parents know their friends and touch base with their friends' parents. It's the whole "it takes a village" philosophy.

A mother from Trinidad tells me that in her community, children wear their school uniforms all the time, and the parents love it. "When a child does something wrong," she says, "we can look at their uniform and tell which school they are coming from." And don't think that moms over there think twice about calling the school to let them know what's up and who's getting into trouble. The school then calls the child's parents, who feel embarrassed and responsible and impress upon the teenager that this behavior is not acceptable. Too many strikes and a kid gets kicked out of school—something most parents are highly motivated to avoid.

You don't have to brand your child with your family crest to have the same effect. Just get to know his friends by name and make an effort to know his friends' parents as well. You want to be in a position where if someone in your teenager's circle is in trouble, you are comfortable calling that teen's parents to let them know, and you'd expect the same of the other parents in your teen's group.

You'll be making your teenager feel responsible for himself, and also accountable to his family. You are impressing upon him that he's not just his own person; he's part of a team, and there are certain expectations that come with that. You'll be giving him a vague but unshakable feeling that whatever he gets involved with will somehow be reported back to you and he'll have to answer for his actions. Given these circumstances, he's far more likely to act as if you're always kind of with him, whispering in his ear, looking out for him and his future.

THE LAST LAST WORD

It's normal for teenagers to separate from their parents, and to want to lead their own lives and make their own choices. It's not good for you or for your relationship with your teen to try to micromanage him and his decisions. But it is up to you to guide your teen as he starts to see life from the angle of a young adult. No matter how strong a community you've formed around your teenager, no one will ever love your child as intensely or protect your child as fiercely as you.

Don't make your teenager wade into adult territory, filled with consequence-laden decisions that can impact his life and the lives of those he touches for decades to come, without a map. Make rules, and don't be afraid to enforce them. Know your teen's friends and their friends' parents, and form a community of people dedicated to making sure all of the teens you all care about stay safe and make smart choices. Ask your teen questions and follow-up questions, and don't worry about seeming uncool. Give your teenager plenty of information and places to get even more information, and then trust your teen to make smart decisions, even when you're not around.

Keep connecting with your teen as your child becomes a young adult; keep revising your view of your teenager and what she understands or is capable of. Your teenager is constantly evolving, and the faster you move to keep up, the more effort you make to stay close, the more positive influence you will be able to exert on your child's life.

Believe me, your teenager will thank you.

A warm and heartfelt thank-you to: all the teenagers and parents who shared their stories, Carol Mann and Laura Yorke at the Carol Mann Agency, John Duff and Marian Lizzi at Perigee, Marisa Nightingale, Sarah Brown, and Bill Albert at The National Campaign to Prevent Teen Pregnancy. To my friends and family who offered your thoughts and your time, my deepest thanks: Atoosa Rubenstein, Rachel Holtzman, Jason Arbuckle, Sadie Van Gelder, Korey Karnes, Caroline Stanley, Tommy Dunne, Rebecca Barry, Pat Volin, Val Weaver, Sean Byrne, Jennifer Braunschweiger, Don and Rosanne Tobey, Sarah Kaatz, Esther, Wendi, Andrew and Mandy, Dan and Patricia. Thanks also to Michael Krameisen, and Gail Milazzo, Michelle Sullivan and Kadidja Hinds, Martine Natasha Johnson, Jason German, Estelle Raboni, Susan Kaplow and Sara Lieberman, Chris Gonzales, and Taylor Thompson.

And to my family, Solins and Weills: Your support is immeasurable.

Sabrina Weill is the former editor-in-chief of *Seventeen* magazine. She was the founding executive editor of *CosmoGIRL!* and editor of Scholastic's teen health magazine *Choices*. She is also the author of *The Seventeen Guide to Sex and Your Body* and *We're Not Monsters: Teens Speak Out About Teens in Trouble*. Weill is a speaker on teens and sex, as well as other issues relating to teenagers (www.sabrinaweill.com). She lives in New York City with her husband, son, and daughter.

Index